EDITED BY THOMAS PATRICK MELADY

WITNESS
TO THE
FAITH

CATHOLICISM AND CULTURE
IN THE PUBLIC SQUARE

GEORGE V. VOINOVICH • ANNE RYDER • LEWIS E. LEHRMAN • REV. MICHAEL SCANLAN
RICK SANTORUM • JOSEPH A. STIBORA • REV. ROBERT SIRICO • MERCEDES WILSON
HELEN M. ALVARE • MICHAEL A. FERGUSON • CHRISTOPHER H. SMITH • ALAN KEYES

Our Sunday Visitor Publishing Division
Our Sunday Visitor, Inc.
Huntington, Indiana 46750

To the memory of
Philip J. Melady and Margaret Miner
who immigrated in the late 1870s
as young people from Ireland and Scotland

and

Adelad Belisle and Marianne Breault
who immigrated from
Quebec Province, Canada
in the late 1890s
and brought with them the faith
that was transmitted to me.

Previous Books by Thomas Patrick Melady

Public Catholicism
Profiles of African Leaders
White Man's Future in Africa
Faces of Africa
Kenneth Kaunda of Africa
Revolution of Color
Western Policy and the Third World
House Divided (co-author)
Development Lessons for the Future (co-author)
Burundi: The Tragic Years
Uganda: The Asian Exiles
Idi Amin: Hitler in Africa (co-author)
The Ambassador's Story
Catholics in the Public Square (editor)

TABLE OF CONTENTS

Foreword

During his October 1995 visit to the United States, our Holy Father spoke thousands upon thousands of words: powerful words, provocative words, moving, encouraging, inspiring, thrilling words. No words, perhaps, were more creative than those addressed to the United Nations, none more exciting than those in the Meadowlands, or more appealing than to the young in Central Park.

Present for all of them, however, listening intently and reviewing them in print, I find them summarized most poignantly in the question the pope asked of New York and all the land at the Aqueduct Raceway, in the Diocese of Brooklyn. "Is there room," he asked, "for the mystery of God?" I quote the passage:

> Dear friends, we are gathered together in this enormous metropolis of New York, considered by many to be the zenith of modern civilization and progress, a symbol of America and American life. For more than 200 years people of different nations, languages, and cultures have come here, bringing memories and traditions of the "old country," while at the same time becoming part of a new nation. America has a reputation the world over, a reputation of power, prestige and wealth. But not everyone here is powerful; not everyone here is rich. In fact, America's sometimes extravagant affluence often conceals much hardship and poverty.
>
> From the viewpoint of the kingdom of God we must therefore ask a very basic question: have the people living in this huge metropolis lost sight of the blessings which belong to the poor in spirit? In the midst of the magnificent scientific and technological civilization of which America is proud . . . is there room for the mystery of God?

I repeat our Holy Father's basic question: "Is there room for the mystery of God?" It seems to me that this question could well serve as at least the subtitle of *Witness to the Faith: Catholicism*

7

and Culture in the Public Square. I suggest that every one of the issues addressed by each of the presenters individually and by all collectively raise the same question: "Is there room for the mystery of God?" If Catholicism has anything to say to culture in the public square, surely it must be by way of answering the pope's question affirmatively; that yes, through Catholicism, there is room or room can be made for the mystery of God.

How else can we enlighten the culture of death, counteract the horrors of abortion, physician-assisted suicide, euthanasia, infanticide? How else can we advance the dignity of the human person, the meaning of womanhood, the indispensability of marriage and family, the right to an education rooted in reason and morality, the abolition of racism and anti-semitism, an understanding that the poor are worth as much to God as the rich, the immigrant as the native; indeed that every human person is sacred?

The mission of the Catholic Campaign for America is to inform Catholics, to enhance public awareness of what is crucial, to assume a prominent and rightful role in American life. Hence, the five themes of the Campaign. They can be stated quite clearly and straightforwardly.

- To inform the culture, media, and political institutions of the beauty, the sheer beauty, of *properly* taught, understood, and applied Catholic teaching;
- To uphold the dignity of women in their unique life-giving and life-affirming capacities to nurture and strengthen and, indeed, to *save* family life;
- To dispel the culture of death by advancing the culture of life;
- To empower individuals and families over bureaucracies, including the state, while committing ourselves to the common good of society;
- To emphasize choice in education to encourage the freedom of families to choose Christian humanism over secularism.

The Catholic Campaign for America, nonsense to the contrary notwithstanding, has no interest in *imposing* Catholic teaching on the United States, nor is it intended as an instrument for religious conversions. The Campaign aims to inform, to alert, and to raise consciousness concerning the magnificent potential of Catholic social teaching for the good of the entire country. That social teaching can restore America's greatness, can help America recover its ideal of "life, liberty, and the pursuit of happiness" for *all*, can bring America to the fulfillment of its dream and its pledge to be "one nation, under God, with liberty and justice for all."

Each of the presentations published here, in its own way, will inspire those who read with care and with open minds and hearts, to make room for the mystery of God.

John Cardinal O'Connor

Introduction

Since 1991, the Catholic Campaign for America has tried to increase the Catholic electorates' influence in formulating public policy and to focus the public's attention on the richness and beauty of Catholic teachings. This has been accomplished through such activities as annual conventions, spiritual rallies, educational press releases, and engaging newsprint articles. As an a 501(c)(3) nonprofit and nonpartisan organization, the Catholic Campaign for America does not endorse political candidates, fund campaigns, or support political parties. The Campaign's mission, as a lay Catholic movement, is to energize and mobilize Catholics to renew their faith and, through that renewal, to help transform American public policy, culture, and society.

Under the direction of a National Board of Directors, a National Committee with over three hundred members, a growing number of local chapters, a National Headquarters in Washington, D.C., made up of a dedicated staff of lay Catholics, the Catholic Campaign for America is centered upon five grass-root themes: 1) to challenge our political institutions, popular culture, and media to embrace Judeo-Christian values and to help infuse them into American public life; 2) to encourage recognition of the dignity of women and to support the unique life-giving and life-affirming role of women in society, asking the Blessed Mother to be inspiration and guide; 3) to encourage legislatures, the judiciary, and other public institutions to respect and defend the institutions of the family, and the "Culture of Life," particularly by encouraging crisis pregnancy support, adoption, and other alternatives to abortion while seeking ultimate legal protection for all human life, from conception until natural death; 4) to help free society, its institutions, and its peoples to better care for others by encouraging government to transfer power from centralized bureaucracies closer to the people; and 5) to enable parents to send their children to the school of their choice.

To accomplish these goals, the Campaign seeks to become the leading lay source of Catholic commentary; to communicate through various media the relevance and importance of Catholic teachings in resolving public policy issues that confront America; and to organize a grass-roots campaign capable of furthering its mission both within the Church and throughout American society. In so doing, the Catholic Campaign for America is consistent with the spirit of the Second Vatican Council, that is, to "renew the temporal order," to be faithful to Christ and the teaching authority of the Magisterium, and to be a witness to the teachings of the Church through sincere dialogue, rational persuasion, and educational mobilization. The Campaign, thus, seeks to mobilize Catholics to become publicly aware and thereby fulfill what it means to be "catholic"—to be universal in faith and in love.

I hope that this book, *Witness to the Faith: The Dialogue of Faith and Culture in the Public Square,* will further discussion of this growing need to become more publicly aware and publicly faithful in our society. The following chapters represent talks presented at our Second Annual National Convention on September 20, 1996, at the Adam's Mark Hotel in Philadelphia, Pennsylvania, and our first-ever Catholic Spiritual Rally on Sunday, September 22, 1996, at the Philadelphia CoreStates Spectrum. Over thirty-five hundred Catholics participated in the weekend events. It was a joyous weekend and a great public witness to the Catholic Faith!

Each of the chapters are edited transcripts. The first part of the book is a series of reflections on "Public Catholicism" in the 1990s. In Chapter I, "Applying the Catholic Vision at the State Level," Governor George V. Voinovich highlights his successes in implementing public policies in the State of Ohio according to our five themes of the Catholic Campaign for America. As the sixty-fifth Governor of Ohio, he is a member of the National Governor's Association Executive Committee and is active in educational reform.

In Chapter II, "Debate in the Public Square: Persuasion Not Coercion," I provide an analysis of the underlying premise of the Catholic Campaign for America — that is, the primacy of the value of rational persuasion over coercion in the public square.

In Chapter III, "The American Founding and the Inalienable Right to Life," Mr. Lewis E. Lehrman, as a recognized expert on national security issues and international affairs, traces the "right to life" in American history and finds common ground between the anti-abortion movement of the 1990s and the anti-slavery movement of the 1860s. Mr. Lehrman is a former Yale University lecturer and holds a master's degree at Harvard University as a Woodrow Wilson Fellow.

In Chapter IV, "Realizing Our Human Potential in the Public Square," Alan Keyes, former Ambassador to the United Nations Economic and Social Council and 1996 Republican presidential nominee, emphasizes the fact that our personhood — our human potential and human essence — is determined absolutely and unconditionally by God, regardless of physical condition and circumstances. Ambassador Keyes is host of "America's Wake-up Call," a nationally syndicated call-in radio talk show. He received both his undergraduate and doctoral degrees in government affairs from Harvard University.

In Chapter V, " 'Hope to Tell' in the Media," Mrs. Anne Ryder describes the challenges of presenting stories of hope and faith on network television news. She is co-anchor of Channel 13 (WTHR), an NBC affiliate in Indianapolis, Indiana. She presents the award-winning "Hope to Tell" series, which recently featured stories on Mother Teresa and Captain Scott O'Grady of the United States Air Force.

In Chapter VI, "Hope in the Public Square," Reverend Michael Scanlan, T.O.R., preaches a message of hope in the future and permanency of the truth. Father Scanlan is president of Franciscan University in Steubenville and in 1990 was awarded the *Cross Pro Ecclesia et Pontifice* by Pope John Paul II. He received the Founders Award from the Fellowship of Catholic Scholars in 1993, and in 1995 was honored by the Pro-Life Action League with the Protector Award for his defense of the unborn. Father Scanlan is a graduate of the Harvard Law School and served as a Staff Judge Advocate in the United States Air Force.

In Chapter VII, "Raising Our Consciences on Partial-Birth Abortion," Senator Rick Santorum of Pennsylvania comments on the vote on the partial-birth abortion bill in the 104th Congress and his personal initiative to educate other members of the Senate on the reality of abortion. Senator Santorum was elected to the

House of Representatives in 1990 and has made his mark fighting for congressional accountability, stressing the need for fiscal responsibility, and contributing to welfare and health care reform.

In Chapter VIII, "Evangelizing in an Increasingly Secular Society," Joseph A. Stibora, director of the *Millennium Evangelization Project* at the University of Dallas, delineates the typical Catholic responses of integrating faith and politics and outlines the authenitc response to John Paul II's call to a Church "re-evangelization" of Western culture. Mr. Stibora, currently a Ph.D. candidate in political philosophy from the University of Dallas, is an active member of the American Political Science Association and the Society of Catholic Social Scientists.

The second part of the book focuses on the Catholic Campaign for America's five campaign themes. In Chapter IX, "Solidarity: A Call to Community," Reverend Robert A. Sirico, C.S.P., expounds his thoughts on the 's teaching of subsidiarity and the working of authority and influence in a political system. Reverend Sirico is co-founder and president of the Acton Institute for the Study of Religion and Liberty. Father Sirico is a member of the Michigan Civil Rights Commission, the Mont Pelerin Society, the American Academy of Religion, the Philadelphia Society, and the Board of Advisors of the Civic Institute in Prague.

In Chapter X, "Upholding the Dignity of Women: Witnessing to the Truth in Istanbul," Mercedes Wilson sketches the recent history of bias against the family and attacks on the dignity of women from family planning organizations in the international arena. Mrs. Wilson also presents the deleterious medical facts of abortion and contraception and the scientific benefits of Natural Family Planning. Mrs. Wilson is president of the Family of the Americas Foundation and chairman of the board of the World Organization of the Family. She served as a Guatemalan delegate to the United Nations Conference on Population and Development in Cairo, Egypt.

In Chapter XI, "Abortion and the Culture of Death," Helen M. Alvare presents the evil of abortion and the culture of death in the context of every human being's right not to be violated or killed by another. She is the director of information and planning for the

Secretariat for Pro-Life Activities for the National Conference of Catholic Bishops. She earned her master's degree in theology at the Catholic University of America and a doctorate of jurisprudence at Cornell Law School.

In Chapter XII, "A Growing Consensus: Choice in Education," Michael A. Ferguson, the executive director of the Catholic Campaign for America, stresses the importance of reclaiming the parental right to choose the education of their children. Mr. Ferguson earned his undergraduate degree from the University of Notre Dame in 1992 and a master's degree in public policy from Georgetown University. He served in several public policy, non-profit, and advisory positions, specializing in educational reform issues.

In Chapter XIII, "Judeo-Christian Values in Politics, Media, and Culture," Congressman Christopher Smith comments on the growing secular humanism in our culture, especially in our political and economic institutions. Congressman Smith represents New Jersey's Fourth Congressional District. In the United States House of Representatives, he serves as vice-chairman of the Veterans Affairs Committee and as chairman of the Subcommittee on International Operations and Human Rights.

I hope that this book will stimulate dialogue on the five themes of the Catholic Campaign for America. Our goal is simply to "Shine the Light — to Believe, Witness, and Evangelize." I am confident that the our witness to the tradition, richness, and goodness of the Catholic Faith will benefit our country, our families, and future generations of Americans.

Thomas P. Melady
Chairman, National Committee
Catholic Campaign for America

Chapter I
Governor George V. Voinovich

Applying the Catholic Vision at the State Level

Recently I read an article from the June 1996 issue of *America* by Peter Schineller about Juan Luis Segundo, an important Jesuit theologian from Uruguay who recently died. Schineller examined Father Segundo's thinking about three questions all of us must face:

Why did God create us?

What is the purpose of my life?

What does God expect of me?

Answers to these questions generally lead to two different world views. In the first, people of faith are exiled to a dangerous world in which their one goal is to avoid the contamination of sin. This world view suggests the world is not our home, that we are pilgrims "restlessly on our way to the Holy City," and that we aren't likely to strike roots here or commit to improving political or cultural situations.

In the second, we are placed in the world to work together with God and one another to transform the earth, build the kingdom and so attain salvation. Father Segundo emphasizes this view, and sees us as ". . . coworkers with God in the mighty project of witnessing to and building the kingdom of God, a kingdom of peace, justice and unity."

Surely most of you, as I do, subscribe to the second view. I am sure you follow the guidance of the Second Vatican Council which clearly suggests that "the laity are called upon to be not simply members of the church, but fruitful members, laboring with God in God's vineyard." I would like to direct my remarks toward this end, and look at how we can address several of the Catholic Campaign's themes by translating that view into "laboring with God in God's vineyard."

The first campaign theme resolves "*To challenge our politi-*

cal institutions, popular culture and media to embrace Judeo-Christian values. . . ." The fact is, societies which are not based on sound religious values are doomed. Faith, family, and community are the bedrocks on which our values, our character, and our moral outlook are built, and this truth, more than ever before, must be shouted from the rooftops, particularly by more Catholics. Too often, we have kept our mouths shut because we have been afraid to step on someone's toes or cross the line between church and state. Thank God the Catholic Church is standing up, along with other religious faiths, against the president's veto of the partial-birth abortion law.

Without our support, I am sure the vote in the House would not have been 285-187 to override it. Unfortunately, few expect the Senate to override the veto. I agree with Senator Dole that this vote defines who we recognize as part of a human family. We passed a similar law in Ohio (H.B. 135 — Luebbers) this year by an overwhelming margin — 28-4 in the Senate and 82-15 in the House. Even "pro-choice" members supported it. And of course, the National Abortion and Reproductive Rights Action League has taken us to court.

This is the second time I have been to Philadelphia this week. I was also at Vila Nova with thirteen governors to hear about Bob Dole's proposals to curb the explosion of drug use by juveniles. Perhaps you've read John J. Dilulio, Jr.'s writing on "The Coming of the Super-Predators." He examines the roots of youthful crime and violence, and one of those roots is moral poverty. Dilulio's solution to youthful crime and violence is simple. "My one big idea," he says, "is borrowed from three well-known child development experts — Moses, Jesus Christ, and Mohammed. It is called religion. If we are to have a prayer of stopping any significant fraction of the super-predators short of the prison gates, then we had better say 'Amen' and fast."

The next campaign theme resolves *"To encourage recognition of the dignity of women and to support the unique life-giving and life-affirming role of women in society, asking the Blessed Mother to be our inspiration and guide."* I am amazed at the number of people I meet who, like me, are devoted to the Blessed Mother and who recite the rosary. For many Catholics of my generation, a strong devotion to Mary was part of our upbringing. The Ursuline nuns and my mom encouraged my personal devotion, and when I attended public high school, I served Sorrowful Mother Novenas on Monday night in my parish church. No one has done more to renew the devotion to our Blessed Mother to be our inspiration and guide than Pope John Paul II. He chose *"Totus Tuus"* as his motto — "I am completely yours, O Mary."

What a wonderful country this would be if every Catholic started each day with the *Memorare*, recited the rosary, and treated every woman (and man) with the same respect we show Our Lady. The Holy Father tells us: "We must return to the figure of Mary — Mary, herself and devotion to Mary when lived out in all its fullest becomes a powerful and creative inspiration." I have tried to use this inspiration in the public policy decisions I have made in Ohio. I believe that we have a fundamental need and moral obligation to cherish, protect, and nurture our families and children. That is why strengthening the family and improving our education system have been at the heart of everything I have tried to do as governor. I have often said that, if I could wave a magic wand to solve our problems in Ohio, I would reconstitute the family.

In my first State of the State Address, I drew a line in the sand for this generation of Ohio's children, and we moved to make this commitment into a measurable goal, which is National Education Goal One: *"By the year 2000, all children in America will start school ready to learn."* We have redefined education in Ohio to mean "lifelong learning," from conception to retirement, understanding that by the time they're between eight and ten years old, children have reached eighty percent of their learning capacity. A recent Carnegie Foundation study has confirmed the importance of early childhood development.

We're accomplishing this through our *Family & Children First* initiative which focuses on three priorities: 1) Expanding access to high quality preschool and child care; 2) increasing family stability; and 3) assuring healthier infants and children. We're putting our money where our hearts are during a period of the lowest growth in state spending in forty years, we have reordered our priorities, and have increased the funding for programs affecting families and children, including education, by thirty-four percent. Ohio will lead the nation in state funding for Head Start by 1998, every eligible child whose family seeks enrollment will be placed in an early childhood program. The Catholic Church is very much a part of our program.

In addition, we are making progress on some other important fronts. The number of fully-immunized two-year-olds is up sixteen percent. Infant mortality rates are down; and state adoption assistance is up two hundred twenty-five percent since 1991. We have reduced adoption-related regulations by twenty-five percent. Our *Family & Children First* initiative evolved from our determination to create the best possible environment for families, an environment that makes support services accessible, and that helps future parents feel confident about the care and the quality of life awaiting their children.

I believe government is one thread in the fabric of a community, and our job is to galvanize all resources to meet the needs of our community. In our efforts *". . . to respect and defend the institutions of the family and the 'Culture of Life,' "* we must take care of those who are unable to take care of themselves, and to help move those who have the ability toward becoming self-sufficient. While we have implemented "tough-love, self-sufficiency" welfare reform and are one of three states to eliminate General Assistance (GA) for able-bodied adults, we have also provided a new program for those who are disabled and are unable to take care of themselves. Today, our Aid to Families and Dependent Children (AFDC) caseload is at its lowest level since 1980, and when our AFDC and GA caseload reductions are combined, we have 305,870 fewer Ohioans on public assistance than during our peak in 1992.

One reason I believe we have been successful is that we have tried to look at welfare recipients not as numbers or case files, but as God's children. I will never forget when we eliminated the first phase of GA and reviewed each person's eligibility. First, many didn't show up. Then we found nearly nine hundred GA recipients who should have been getting $430 every month in Supplemental Security disability benefits instead of $141 from us. For able-bodied individuals, we think the best welfare solution is a job. We have worked hard to create a favorable business climate, and today, Ohio is blessed with a strong economy that has produced thousands of jobs. Ohio was ranked first among all states in new and expanded business facilities for the third year in a row, and our unemployment rate is at a twenty-year low.

If you really want to do something for society, create more jobs. I say three things to the business people who ask me what they can do to help — make money, create jobs, and pay taxes. We have put initiatives in place that have made it possible for many Ohio families to leave the welfare roles and enter the workforce. Our Job Opportunity and Basic Skills (JOBS) program has helped put thousands of Ohioans to work. In fact, Ohio leads the nation in the number of AFDC recipients participating in the JOBS program — forty-six percent take part in it as of the state's 1996 fiscal year.

In addition to the training and "job-readiness" aspects of our welfare reform package, we have included some "common-sense" changes that will strengthen families. For example, mothers and fathers on public assistance will no longer be punished for being married or obtaining part-time jobs. Teenage mothers must live with a responsible adult to receive public assistance, and the parents of a teenage father can now be held liable for child support for their grandchild. We have also cracked down hard on child-support enforcement. From 1991 through 1995, Ohio's total child-support collections increased by forty-one percent to $1.24 billion. The nonpayment of child support is a national scandal. At least half of the families on public assistance in Ohio are there because the noncustodial parent doesn't pay child support. This is no less than government-approved financial child abuse, and we must make it as socially unacceptable as we have made drinking and driving.

As we have done in Ohio with our *Family & Children First* and our welfare reform initiatives, I encourage all of you to help develop local, "homegrown" solutions that are tailored to the needs and the resources of your community. I think this is an important dimension of "laboring with God in God's vineyard." This is also why we support the Personal Responsibility and Work Opportunity Act that Congress passed last July 30, and the president signed into law in August. With our *Family & Children First* initiative up and running in all eighty-eight Ohio counties, we will now have the flexibility to design services and move resources around to take care of special or multiple-needs families, and we are able to contract with local providers, nonprofit organizations, and others to help tailor the services to local needs. Incidentally, when Ohio was one of two states NGA's *Family & Children First* conference in Baltimore last year, I was very irritated when the president said that he and the faceless bureaucrats in Washington care more about families and children than we do at the state and local levels.

I would like to look for a moment at the part of the campaign theme that encourages "*. . . alternatives to abortion while seeking ultimate legal protection for all human life. . . .*" Those of us who accept the "Culture of Life" see the abortion issue as a matter of conscience and a matter of our most sacred personal beliefs. So often people come up to me to thank me for my pro-life stand. My response is that I need no thanks — for me it's a matter of my immortal soul. Unfortunately, the Supreme Court reaffirmed *Roe* v. *Wade* in the Casey decision, and this is not likely to change any-time soon. In addition, President Clinton — by executive order — overturned almost every abortion restriction from the Reagan-Bush era within days of taking office.

In Ohio we have pursued aggressive legislative and administrative remedies to limit abortion within the boundaries of *Roe* v. *Wade*. I already mentioned that I signed legislation which bans dilation and extraction abortions in Ohio. Our "parental notification" law became effective in November of 1991. In August of 1991, I signed the "women's right to know" bill (H.B. 108 — Luebbers) into law which imposes a twenty-four-hour waiting period for women seeking an abortion and requires abortion providers to share information about fetal development and abortion alternatives. We make sure they do it. In May of this year, I signed legislation (S.B. 239 — Nein) making it a crime to injure or kill a viable fetus. This came about when an Ohio woman who was eight-and-a-half months pregnant was killed in a car accident. The county prosecutor had been unable to secure two counts of vehicular homicide because a fetus, prior to this bill, had not been defined as a person.

I already mentioned our increased financial support for adoption services. We have also reformed the state's adoption laws. The new law standardizes adoption practice across all of Ohio's eighty-eight counties, decreases the time a child waits for a permanent home, enacts safeguards for all the parties involved in an adoption, and clarifies access to adoption information. It wouldn't have happened without National Right to Life and the United States Catholic Conference, both of which guided us through the adoption reform "land mines." Simply put, we are trying to create a family-friendly environment where expectant mothers know that the very best care is available to them and their babies, and where women who do not want or can't care for their babies know that Ohio's adoption program is one of the best anywhere. It is working — our most recent statistics show four thousand fewer abortions in 1995 than in 1994 in Ohio.

The next campaign theme resolves *"To help free society, its institutions, and its people to better care for others by encouraging government to transfer power from centralized bureaucracies closer to the people."* Our nation's forefathers referred to this as "federalism," and outlined our relationship in the Tenth Amendment: *"The power not delegated to the United States by the Constitution, nor prohibited by the states, are reserved to the states respectively, or to the people."*

I contend that the power now residing in Washington, D.C., should never have gone there in the first place. I sincerely believe that unless power is returned to the states and to the people, we will never get the federal government off our backs and our of our pockets. To that end, I led the charge last year to get Bob Dole's Senate Bill 1 (unfunded mandates relief legislation) passed. Returning power to the states, or the "devolution" of power from the federal government, was the goal behind the unfunded mandates relief legislation. That new law represents a "paradigm shift," and one of the most significant changes in the way the federal government does business in decades. We have finally canceled Congress's credit card to charge state and local governments with the projects they do not want to pay for themselves. The other significant legislation which moved devolution further is the ending of welfare as a federal entitlement. "Empowerment" is what this is all about.

If we truly want *". . . to help free society, its institutions, and its people to better care for others,"* then we have got to get control of the federal deficit and balance the budget. In 1985, the deficit was $1.7 trillion. Today, it's $5 trillion. The interest we pay on the debt will exceed what we pay for national defense; it's eight times what we invest in education; it's 50 times what we spend on job training, and it's 145 times what we pay for childhood immunizations. If we do not take care of the deficit, there simply will not be anything left for anyone, especially the least of our brothers and sisters. I am a deficit "hawk," but I support Bob Dole's 15 percent tax cut and the job creation capital gains tax cut. It'll never be done without a Republican House and Senate.

The final campaign theme resolves *"To enable parents to send their children to the school of their choice."* First of all, as a former mayor of Cleveland and as current governor of Ohio, I would like to express my gratitude to those of you who are involved with non-public education. Our non-public schools, especially in urban areas, have provided thousands of children — many of them non-Catholic minorities — with the chance to develop their God-given talents so they can take care of themselves and their families and make a contribution to society.

That chance is especially important while we put forth a "full-court press" to improve our urban school systems. Next to the federal deficit, I consider the measurable improvement of our urban school districts to be our greatest challenge. And while we are fixing public education, we need to build up — not tear down — our non-public school system. It is time more Catholics stood up for it. I am proud that, of the thirteen states providing substantive support for non-public schools, Ohio leads the nation on a per-pupil basis ($138 million / $599 per pupil). I encourage those of you who live in states that do not provide support for non-public schools to lobby your elected officials. Remind them that in 1977, state laws permitting public funds to provide private schools with things like textbooks, lab equipment, transportation, and computer software was, in part, declared constitutional by the U.S. Supreme

Court. Of course, the Supreme Court prohibited public support that could be diverted to religious use.

I am very grateful that, thanks to Bishop Pilla's leadership, all thirty-two Cleveland Catholic schools volunteered to be part of our "school choice" pilot project — the first of its kind in the nation in which parents are permitted to enroll their children in parochial schools. That pilot project — the "Cleveland Scholarship and Tutoring Program" — has awarded scholarships to nearly two thousand low-income Cleveland children in grades K-3. The program is expected to continue through their eighth grade year. Our emphasis is on helping low-income families. Three of every four children enrolled in the program live at the poverty level. However, we also require these families to pay ten percent of the scholarship, which might include in-kind services to the school. The state is extending a hand, but the parents have a stake as well.

School choice will not cure all our educational problems, but I believe it will go a long way toward ensuring competition and increasing diversity in our schools. I support Bob Dole's school choice initiative, and so should you. I am tired of the AFT [American Federation of Teachers] and the NEA [National Education Association] standing in the way of reforming our education system. It is ironic that, in Cleveland, where the AFT is still fighting, thirty-five percent of the teachers send *their* kids to private schools.

The next several years promise to challenge our society. We have before us the opportunity for the public and private sectors to work together and galvanize our resources. It will be a special time for leaders in the Church, in government, and in every field of endeavor. How well we do will depend on your willingness to promote the Catholic Campaign for America's five themes in your respective states and communities.

There are lots of governors throughout the country like George Voinovich who need your help. For example, we never would have been able to get our benchmark "school choice" program for nonpublic schools through the legislature without an individual named Dave Brennan, who headed up my educational choice commission, and helped me lobby for our legislation. One person can make a difference. I would like to leave you with my two mottoes. The first is my personal motto from my days as mayor of Cleveland: "Together we can do it." The second is Ohio's state motto: "With God, all things are possible." I am confident that, with God's help and together, we will fulfill Father Segundo's challenge to labor ". . . with God in building the kingdom through love of neighbor."

I hope you leave this convention with the words from one of my favorite hymns — "God's blessing sends us forth, strengthened for our task on Earth, refreshed in soul, renewed in mind, may God with us remain, and through us His Spirit reign that Christ be known to all mankind."

Chapter II
Thomas P. Melady

Debate in the Public Square: Persuasion Not Coercion

Most of us believe in a set of values that have been given to us. We love and we embrace these values. We want to advocate them in the public square. We hope to convince others to embrace these values. I want to see us do it with enthusiasm and with courtesy, politeness, and respect for others. Nowhere today are common courtesy, respectful dialogue, and regard for each other more absent than in our public square. Poll after poll shows that Americans fear that incivility has become the new rage in civil debate and that we are abusing the freedoms and religious values that bind us into one nation under God.

As religious Americans we face a dilemma. On one hand, some religious Americans are loath to speak about religion for fear of imposing their beliefs on others. On the other hand, some religious Americans seem to lash out at others with self-righteous rhetoric. Yet as Catholic Americans, neither path is compatible with our history nor heritage.

And so it is appropriate that we gather together today in Philadelphia, in the city of brotherly love, to renew our commitment to our country and to our mission as Catholics, to practice dignified debate in the public square and in our discourse with our neighbors who may have another point of view. When our founding fathers sought freedom of speech and worship, they came here to Philadelphia. When our founding fathers brought forth upon this continent a new nation, they conceived of its liberties and values here in Philadelphia. This city is where our Liberty Bell first rang. Philadelphia is where our Declaration of Independence still rests. And so in Philadelphia, we declare today, a different way, a new way, a Catholic way, to and through the public square. This way is built on respect for others. It is built on the roots of our Catholic heritage. And it is built upon the cornerstone of our American and Catholic commitment to family, to community, and to country.

As Catholic Americans we are encouraged by the U.S. Constitution and covenant to champion our values in the public square. Yet our methods must promote civil discourse and dialogue. For it is only under such conditions that democracy can flower and flourish. And politeness has been and should remain an intrinsic part of Catholic culture. Core Catholic beliefs have been transmitted to us by our Church leaders. An historic part of Catholic culture has been respect for the pope and his fellow bishops. And Catholic Americans have been faithful to this tradition of solidarity with our Church leadership. Catholic Americans have also been loyal to the American tradition of energetically participating in public discourse. Like many good things in America, our first lessons about democracy, civil discourse, and the public square begin at home. I can often recall my mother saying to me, "Tommy, the path to wisdom begins when our mouths are closed and our ears are open." And, in part, our common path to the public square should begin in that same way. Sometimes we need to listen more and talk less. It is often easier to shout at one another than listen to one another. And today, there are too many shrill voices in the public arena. But America demands more from us than that. America gives each and every American the right to debate and defend those beliefs in the public forum.

Because of that sacred right, the public square will always be a place for passionate dialogue. But it should never be a place for harsh voices or violence. It should never be a place for mean remarks about fellow citizens who hold other points of view. We should be clear and firm in what we believe. But, good Christians should not be "attack dogs" in opposing other viewpoints.

America rests on the premise that Americans can decide what is best for them when given the time to converse and to reflect with each other. Yet, as we know, coercion is no substitute for reflection. *Our goal in contemporary America should be to persuade through reason, dialogue and prayer.*

There is no question that some of the issues facing us energize basic moral questions. The protection of life from conception to natural death, for example, has become a burning contemporary challenge to our basic beliefs. In defending these beliefs it is easy to return emotional negative rhetoric with the same or even worse.

But we should refrain from doing that. While remaining faithful to our core Catholic teachings and doing all that we can to persuade our fellow citizens to accept them, we should never engage in mean-spirited debate, name calling, or even worse, the use of violence.

Perhaps the best example of shared dialogue I can offer comes from my time in Rome. As some of you know, I served as Ambassador to the Vatican during the Gulf War. But as some of you may not know, officials in the Vatican and U.S. Catholic Church leaders had different opinions on how to respond to the conflict. One day I discussed the matter with two leading churchmen who had opposing views on this life-and-death issue. Both were devoted to the pope and his teaching authority.

As an envoy of the United States, I supported President Bush's decision to use military force against Iraq. One Church leader with whom I spoke shared my position, but on the same day another Church leader argued that all human life was sacred and that even Sadaam Hussein's "naked aggression" did not justify waging military action in Kuwait. At times our words grew as pointed and sharp as the dark-roast espresso that one drinks in Rome. Even though no one's mind had really been changed, still, we were able to respect each other, to listen to each other, and to come away from that experience with a greater perspective on war and peace in the Persian Gulf.

That same sense of respect is what we need in America today. Our country has always valued religious and political diversity. We even enshrine it on our coins with the motto "*E Pluribus Unum*" — Out of Many, One.

It is this fundamental respect and acceptance of the Constitution that gives our society the civilized framework where we can discuss our differences. Respect forms the common ramparts of morality around our pluralistic public square. Respect springs from a profound regard for the personhood of others. And it is this profound regard for the personhood of others that forms the cornerstone of our democracy and the golden rule of our faith.

Yet respect alone is not enough. Respect provides the context for our debate. But our unique Catholic heritage has much more to offer to the content and character of our campaign in the public square.

Father Richard Neuhaus speaks eloquently of the naked public square in America and the dawn of a Catholic moment needed to clothe it. He warns us that the liberal left has stripped every vestige and vestment of religious cloth from the American public square. Others warn that the religious right has gone public with its religion, often proclaiming the Sacred Scriptures from public pulpits, yet not explaining the wisdom of the Sacred Scriptures which makes them accessible to all. And so we come to a crossroads on our way to the public square.

Ours is a different way. It is the Catholic way. It is the way Robert Frost calls the road less traveled, and this road runs right down the middle of the public square. Our model for the way to evangelize should be the way of the Holy Father, whose view is always crystal clear on *what should be,* and he refrains from attacking those who do not embrace our beliefs. Our method for evangelizing should avoid the extremes of rhetoric. We should choose the way of rational persuasion. The great persuader of the second half of this century is Pope John Paul II.

Granted, forceful but courteous dialogue is often where extremists refuse to tread. Yet being clear, forthright, and courteous is not a sign of weakness. It is a sign of strength. It takes considerable restraint, reasoning, humility, and faith.

We know that the gospel shows us the way to the truth and the light. And as Catholics we know that we have the pope and the bishops to guide us in the application of the gospel of Jesus to contemporary life. But we must share the light as well as shine the light, and we must discuss our ways to truth in a dignified dialogue.

We know that the truth will make us free, but freedom is the recognition that no one has a monopoly on how to apply God's truth to every societal situation. Freedom is the recognition that every individual is precious, that every one of us has been put here for a reason, and that every one of us has something to offer in the public square.

Although the path of civil dialogue is often less traveled, others in our Church have blazed a trail for us. In the days of the Roman Empire, our Church was a small, persecuted faith. Roman law required Christians to worship the emperor, which, of course, was something they could not do.

However, the Christian philosopher Origen was able to appeal to a Roman custom and win religious amnesty for our Christian forefathers. In antiquity, standards of value were different from today; back then, the older something was, the better it was.

In this Roman period of history, Origen was able to go before Emperor Theodotian and reason with him. Origen demonstrated to the emperor that Christianity's roots ran as deep into the common soil of human history as Rome's did. Theodotian quickly granted all Christians freedom of worship.

As we evangelize and spread the light of our faith, we will confront practices which contradict core Catholic teachings on life from conception to natural death, the family right for school choice, social justice for the poor, capital punishment, and war and peace. Some who are opposed to our teachings will attack us in ways and terms that are not in accordance with the traditions of civilized discourse. Our response, however, should be in accordance with our Catholic and American traditions. We will *patiently* and *politely* try to persuade. We will not return an ugly remark with one of our own. And as I previously noted, we will never return violence with violence.

Following the example of Pope John Paul II on his visits to all corners of the earth, we must be crusaders and campaigners in the public square. But, like the Holy Father, we must also be ambassadors and explorers in the public square. We must believe, witness, and evangelize. But, we must also reach out, bring together, and build up.

Our Catholic ancestors in the nineteenth century and the early decades of the twentieth century suffered from some forms of prejudice because they came as immigrants with a religion that was strange to the predominant American Protestant communities of that period.

However, core values of the American public in the nineteenth and early twentieth centuries coincided with fundamental Catholic values on the family and respect for life. Today Catholics in the United States have a new challenge: significant numbers of our fellow citizens have other positions on these issues that are contrary to our fundamental beliefs.

What should be our course of action? It must fit into the constitutional framework — *persuasion*. It should be done in a calm, cool, and courteous fashion. Faithful to our fundamental teachings we must avoid shrill-voiced name-calling, as it is not true to our Catholic tradition. Furthermore, it is not productive in a democratic society.

We know the way to increase our influence so that our ideas and recommendations reflecting our Catholic heritage will have a greater impact on the discussions in the public square.

We should be respected because we are good citizens serving society in our local communities, in the state, and in the nation. The more we participate in a positive, creative way in our community, the more influence we will have on all issues.

Many voices invoked at this convention remind us of how our Catholic values are sewn into the very fit and fabric of American democracy. Thomas Jefferson reminds us that the common truths we hold "self-evident" stem from "Nature and Nature's God." Cardinal James Gibbons reminds us that no political document so resonates with Catholic values as does our Constitution. Father John Courtney Murray reminds us that Catholicism is compatible with democracy, and we must insure that our democracy also remains compatible with Catholicism.

Yes, I believe, like the road less traveled, we Catholics have an unnoticed gift to give to our country. That is our unwavering ability to build family and community. Nothing receives or deserves more attention today than family values. This phrase falls off politicians' lips until it is little more than a meaningless slogan.

Yet, has not our Church been a family since its conception? Does not our Holy Father, Pope John Paul II, enshrine the family at the heart of the culture of life? And do not Catholic families all over the world celebrate family values each Sunday at Mass, and do not parents kneel with their children in nightly prayer?

As Catholics, our family ties stretch even over oceans and behind ethnic lines. This was no more evident to me than when I served as ambassador to Burundi. My first Sunday there I went to Mass in a humble chapel etched into the sultry African rain forest. As I knelt in prayer, I could not help but notice how different our traditions were. We were separated by heritage and history. Nevertheless, we were still all part of one family of faith. We still came together to worship the same God. And we all shared a profound respect for each other. I still remember that Sunday. I still see it as a humble yet poignant example of our Catholic vocation in the American public square.

Despite our differences, within the Catholic family, the Catholic Church remains one community. Our pews are spangled with faces of different color and populated by people from diverse lands, yet we have been, are, and always will be one big family. Sometimes, it seems like we are losing that sense of family in America today. Sometimes it seems the multicolored patchwork of our American quilt is coming apart at the seams. And that is where we Catholics can offer our insight and experience.

When our Church was even younger than our democracy is today, it too faced questions of diversity. The first Christians did not all share a common background. They spoke different languages and hailed from countries often hostile to each other.

Yet just when the infant Church seems to be coming apart at its seams, St. Paul comes on the scene. He identifies a common set of beliefs and calls these beliefs a cornerstone. This cornerstone was so powerful that it united Greek and Roman, Jew and Gentile, slave and free. This cornerstone enabled them to inhabit one Body and empowered them to become one Body. Today, we are still that one Body; we are still that one community; and we are still that one family.

Now, I am not saying we should try to unify America by forcing everyone into our Church or by imposing our beliefs. But, I am suggesting that Paul's example of finding a common set of beliefs holds value for us today. As American Catholics, we too must cast our Catholic cornerstones of the dignity of the human person and of our commitment to community and family, before all to see and on which we all can build. This is how we can help stitch together our American coat of many colors. And this is how we can clothe the naked public square with it. This is how we can hasten the dawn of a Catholic moment in America. And this is how we can all become one country, one community, one family again.

And in conclusion, I challenge each one of us to help do just that. When we return to our homes, hometowns, and town squares, we will encounter disagreement and dissonance over the content and character of our culture. This dissonance may sound in our homes or on the job. It may sound in our town councils or parish councils. It may even sound among friends and family.

But, wherever dissonance does sound, I challenge you to take the road less traveled and travel into the midst of the debate. I challenge *you not to throw stones at each other, but to cast cornerstones with each other*. I challenge you to pick one old issue and get as many new facts as you can about it. I challenge you to study it. I challenge you in particular to listen to people who support the sides of this issue you oppose. And if you still disagree with them when they are through speaking — call them on it. I challenge you to discuss and defend your values — after all, that is a very American thing to do. But I also challenge you to be patient, to pray, and to value each other as members of the same family — after all, that is a very Catholic thing to do.

That is how we can renew our faith and renew the face of our country. And that is what our Catholic Campaign for America is all about. That is our mission. And this is our moment.

Chapter III
Lewis E. Lehrman

The American Founding and the Inalienable Right to Life

"You say that you think slavery is wrong, but you denounce all attempts to restrain it. Is there anything else that you think wrong, that you are not willing to deal with as wrong? Why are you so careful, so tender of this one wrong and no other?" (Abraham Lincoln)

One hundred thirty-five years ago American law held that all human beings are created equal — *except* for black human beings. Today, American law holds that all human beings are equal — *except* for the child-about-to-be-born. But there has been a change. Until recently, abortion was a legal issue, tried before the Supreme Court. But it is now a political struggle — to be tried before the bar of American public opinion. No one, *nothing*, shall be exempt from this struggle, neither courts, nor Congress, nor the presidency.

This is so because *Roe* v. *Wade* ignited a life and death struggle. Americans will end this struggle by resolving crucial issues of fundamental law. First, are the liberals right when they declare the American Constitution to be merely what Supreme Court justices say it to be? Or, instead, is it true that all American citizens are bound to the original interpretations of our organic law, authored by the founders of our country — Thomas Jefferson, James Madison, George Washington? We remember that the founders, in the Declaration of Independence, appealed to "the laws of nature and of nature's God." The American people, on July 4, 1776, anticipating great sacrifice of blood and treasure, declared, in the founding law of the new nation, that "We hold these truths to be self-evident" — "that all men are created equal"; that they "are endowed by their Creator" with the inalienable right to life . . . to liberty . . . to the pursuit of happiness. . . . This is what the founders said; and this is what they meant.

By invoking the binding laws of nature and of nature's God,

the founders of our country implied that any law, any judicial ruling which violates inalienable human rights is, by its nature, unacceptable, indeed unconstitutional since, according to the very words of the Declaration of Independence, it is primarily "to secure these [inalienable human] rights" that "governments are instituted among men." Furthermore, the Declaration specifies that government holds only "just powers derived from the consent of the governed." And moreover, "that whenever any form of government becomes destructive of these ends [namely, the inalienable rights to life and to liberty], it is the right of the people to alter or abolish [that government], and to institute new government." For the founders, an unjust law was no law at all.

Thus, it is fitting to ask a simple and decisive question: Are not all Americans, and their governments — past, present, and future — required by fundamental law to uphold the American doctrine of the inalienable right to life, promulgated in the Declaration of Independence and codified in Amendments V and XIV of the Constitution of the United States? Do these words still have the force of law? As we consider this question, who can honestly ignore the *fact* that it was not only Thomas Jefferson, but also James Madison, the father of the Constitution, who held the Declaration of Independence to be "the fundamental act of American union" — the organic law in virtue of which the union of the colonies was consummated and the American nation inaugurated? Indeed, even today, the Declaration of Independence is placed first in the United States Code of Laws — even ahead of the Constitution.

Thus, we can rightly say again, adapting Mr. Lincoln's own words, that the ancient, the durable, the great moral issue in America has always been the struggle to uphold the Declaration of Independence — and, in our time, to restore the primacy of the inalienable right to life of the child-in-the-womb. This national debate will be resolved either for the arbitrary judge-made right to abort a "*foetus*," a Latin word, of the neuter gender, designed to reduce a child, like the slave, to the status of a nonhuman chattel. Or, on the contrary, Americans will embrace again their fundamental law and restore the inalienable right to life of the child-about-to-be-born who is not a *foetus*, but a human person, the inalienable right to life of whom is protected by the Declaration of Independence and the Constitution of the United States.

It is true that some Supreme Court justices, basing their opinion on the *Cooper* v. *Aaron* decision of 1958, maintain that the law is merely what the Supreme Court says it to be. But, if historically understandable and even legal in some technical sense, can it ever be legitimate for Supreme Court justices to decide for the *permanent* chattel right to hold a Negro as property, a transparently prochoice doctrine, called by the Douglas Democrats of the 1850s "popular sovereignty." Popular sovereignty was nothing but the free choice to make a black man into a slave. Can it now be legitimate to uphold a permanent right to dispose of chattel property in the child-about-to-be-born (now called "pro-choice," merely the modern synonym for slave-holder popular sovereignty, i.e., the free choice to destroy the child-in-the-womb)? If "popular sovereignty" or "pro-choice" doctrines lead to extra-constitutional court decisions, which permanently violate the inalienable human rights of the Declaration and the Constitution, are we to suppose there can be no further appeal?

To this question Mr. Lincoln gave an unflinching answer; and, through a great trial of arms, ending in 1865 with Amendment XIII abolishing slavery, the American people settled the matter *forever*. Today, this very same question of fundamental principle has arisen in the form of the abortion debate. Unlike slavery, this issue shall not be resolved on the battlefield, in the law schools, nor even in the Supreme Court; but instead, in the democratic arena of American politics. This must be so because, in the struggle between the inalienable rights of the Declaration and the *spurious* opinions of *renegade* judges, only we the people, American citizens duly assembled, will ultimately decide.

So it is time to ask sincere advocates of abortion rights: How important is it that, in the unequivocal language of the Fifth and Fourteenth Amendments of the Constitution we find explicit affirmation of the right to life, to liberty, and to property — upheld in that order? Does one deny the plain meaning of the actual sequence of the very words themselves — *first* life, *then* liberty, *then* property? Does one sincerely deny that human liberty is made for human life, not human life for liberty? Must not the correct sequence be self-evident in virtue of biological necessity? Is it to be reasonably supposed, in principle, that the right to liberty can be safe, if the right to life be not secure? Can one maintain intelligibly that human life — "endowed by the Creator" as the Declaration tells us — commences at the hand of the Creator in the sixth month of life, or in the tenth month of life, and not at the very beginning of the life of the child-about-to-be-born? Finally, does one really suppose that the right to life of the child in the womb, an inalienable right secured by the Declaration, may be eviscerated by an extra-constitutional coup of the Supreme Court, acting alone, without direct warrant from the American people who did ordain the Constitution and who, alone, are authorized to amend it? Do the Justices repudiate what our forefathers wrote into the primordial law of the Republic that only "We the people of the United States, in order to form a more perfect Union . . . do ordain this Constitution for the United States of America"?

Given no other means of redress, under present circumstances, there is left to us but one response to the Supreme Court's sponsorship of the unrestrained abortion power. We, the people of the United States, must ourselves reverse the Court. This is urgent and necessary, I say, because the Supreme Court has, through its abortion opinions, overturned the essential principle of the American republic. But how may Americans reverse the Court and restrict abortion, even without a constitutional amendment? Liberals argue, since the Casey decision, that the Supreme Court has finally settled the matter — with few restraints — in favor of abortion-on-demand. Liberal elites and some Supreme Court justices, echoing the 1857 *Dred Scott* opinion, even argue that two decades of pro-abortion Supreme Court rulings are themselves the supreme laws of the land.

Americans have generally responded with respect for Supreme Court holdings in particular cases. But, to ask the American people, the sovereign national authority, to be quiet about first principles of the Constitution, no, never. And furthermore, one may reasonably deny that the Supreme Court can, by itself, permanently decide the supreme law of the land, in matters of fundamental constitutional principle. And, as authority for this opinion, one relies, among others, upon President Thomas Jefferson and President Andrew Jackson — the founders of the Democratic Party. It was Jefferson who wrote, "to consider [Supreme Court] Justices as the ultimate arbiters of all constitutional questions [is] a very dangerous doctrine indeed, and one which would place us under the despotism of an oligarchy." Moreover, he emphasized, "the Constitution has erected no such single tribunal." A generation later, President Jackson, in a dispute with the Supreme Court, declared, "the opinion of judges has no more authority over Congress than the opinion of Congress has over the judges."

And now, let us consider the greatest of our presidents. Mr. Lincoln fiercely rejected the history, the argument, and the *principle* grounding the Supreme Court's decision in the incendiary *Dred Scott* case, an infamous ruling Lincoln refused to accept as a permanent rule of political action. Rendered for the Supreme Court by Chief Justice Roger B. Taney, the *Dred Scott* opinion of 1857 declared, against all Congressional precedent, that slavery could not be prohibited by Congress in any territory of the U.S., that (under the Constitution) the black man could *never* be an American citizen. Moreover, wrote Chief Justice Taney, the black man was a "mere article of merchandise"; the Negro was not included in the language of the Declaration of Independence; indeed, the Chief Justice of the U.S. announced that the black man was "a being of a different order" and had "no rights which the white man was bound to respect." In the words of the 1857 Supreme Court, the Negro, like the child in the womb of the 1973 Supreme Court, was *not* a person. Indeed, Senator Stephen Douglas insisted against private citizen Lincoln, in the great debates of 1858, that the earthly fate of the black man had been confined by the Supreme Court to the property clause of the American Constitution, where, instead of a person, the black man had become, under a Supreme Court ruling, the mere appendage of his master, a chattel — a living mockery of the inalienable right to liberty.

Today, much of the liberal intelligentsia argues in support of Justice Blackmun in *Roe* v. *Wade*, just as Taney did of the Negro in *Dred Scott*, that the child-about-to-be-born is *not* a person, but an appendage in the womb, and thus not protected under the Fifth and Fourteenth Amendments. Justice Blackmun, in his *notorious* opinion on behalf of the abortion power, might just as well have said, paraphrasing the Supreme Court opinion of 1857, on behalf of the slave power, that the child-in-the-womb is also a "mere article of merchandise . . . . a being of a different order," having no rights which American fathers and mothers are bound to respect. Shorn of euphemisms, this, in truth, is their astounding proposition. But in the end, there are two elementary biological findings of fact which falsify this revolting opinion. First, the full human person is actually present in the human embryo from the very first moment of conception. This scientific fact of DNA design is incontestable in reasonable debate. Indeed, it is medically precise to say that the so-called "potential" human life of the 1973 Supreme Court decision is present in a specific human sperm and a specific human egg *before* union. We can see clearly that, just as Chief Justice Taney argued in 1857 that the *Negro* was a "being of a different order," a slave-holder biological theory designed to rationalize the wrong of slavery, so also did the Supreme Court opinion of 1973 rationalize the wrong of abortion by means of fictitious theories of "potential life."

The truth is abortion, in principle, may in fact be *worse* than slavery, an argument as plausible as the truth of the proposition that every human life, black or white, must first be secure that liberty might be enjoyed, an idea best expressed by saying that in the battle of *Roe* v. *Wade*, we deal not only with life and liberty, as in *Dred Scott*, but with life and death.

That both Chief Justice Taney and Justice Blackmun, in rendering their opinions, relied not only on false biological theories, but also on false American history, should *never* be forgotten. Contrary to Taney's recitation of American history, blacks *were* truly citizens at the birth of the Constitution in 1789, voting in at least five states, including the slave-state of North Carolina, for and against ratification of the Constitution. And in 1857, Negroes were still recognized as lawful citizens in several states, despite Taney's ruling in *Dred Scott* that Negroes were not, and could not be, American citizens.

Similarly, the child-in-the-womb was also treated as a person in state law and in federal law at the very moment of the ratification of the Fourteenth Amendment in 1868, the constitutional amendment which secured legal personhood for the Negro. Thus, by their actions, and I believe, by their intent, the congressional lawmakers who framed the Fourteenth Amendment, implicitly included the child-in-the-womb in the due process and in the equal protection clauses of that Amendment. Indeed, before *Roe* v. *Wade* and since, the unborn child was and still is treated, in certain tort and negligence law, explicitly as a human person — all this, under the same Constitution which Justice Blackmun announced in 1973 did not recognize the personhood of the unborn child.

Moreover, in its 1973 opinion, the Supreme Court sidestepped the *fact* that when the Fourteenth Amendment of 1868 was passed, twenty-eight of thirty-seven states held abortion to be a criminal act *prior* to "quickening," two by common law, the remainder by statute. Over the next fifteen years, seven more states made abortion a criminal act. By 1973, when a runaway U.S. Supreme Court fabricated the spurious right to abortion, most states had for generations restricted abortion. For all those who have eyes to see and ears to hear, there was only one historical truth in 1868, at the time of the drafting of the Fourteenth Amendment. It was this: a consensus in law of the American people *did* exist — namely, to restrict abortion. And those politicians who today plead for *no* action, because they say there is *no* consensus, cannot repeal the undeniable consensus in law which did exist, not only in 1868 but also in 1973.

To unmask the false Supreme Court opinion in *Roe* v. *Wade*, it is necessary to explain to the American people that the same Congresses, which prohibited slavery in the Fourteenth Amendment, explicitly incorporated into federal law, at about the same time, criminal codes restricting abortion. For example, Congress restricted abortion on all federal properties located within the states and the territories. Congress *did* this by incorporating very restrictive state anti-abortion laws *directly* into the federal criminal codes of 1859 and 1874, a fact which shows that when Congress resolved the issue of slavery in the Thirteenth, Fourteenth, and Fifteenth Amendments, Congress at the very same time was restricting abortion by federal law. This unexamined but inescapable historical link, between the Congressional abolition of slavery and restriction of abortion, *cannot* be overemphasized. And it was no mere coincidence that the two occurred together. It is worth recalling that the *final* slavery crisis occurred during the 1850s, just as the American Medical Association had successfully carried out a campaign to restrict abortion in the states and the territories. The AMA undertook this campaign in the 1820s and the 1830s because the science of embryology had demonstrated that the life of the child began at the first moment of conception. Indeed, this scientific position the AMA upheld until the 1960s and thus it was written into most medical textbooks. The AMA leaders, before the Civil War, honoring the physicians oath "to do no harm," insisted on presenting the medical facts of embryology to the American people, and they carried this research into its legislatures. From about 1853 to 1883 the state legislatures rigorously restricted abortion because, as the AMA testified in almost every state and territorial legislature, the evidence of the new science of embryology showed that the child is alive in the womb from conception. At the very time the anti-slavery movement was cresting, state legislation restricting abortion was being designed with the express purpose of protecting the child-about-to-be-born, *not*, as Justice Blackmun speciously argued in *Roe* v. *Wade*, to protect the health of the mother — even though it is surely true that the health of the mother should be protected by restricting abortion.

To explain to the American people the history of the parallel anti-slavery and anti-abortion movements should be sufficient intellectual armor to wreck the remaining rotting timbers holding up the Supreme Court's rickety framework fabricated in *Roe* v. *Wade*; and to rewrite the false story, recited by Justice Blackmun in his scandalous 1973 opinion. The truth is, state legislatures concluded during the nineteenth century that the child in the womb, like every other person, had to be protected by all reasonable means, which meant, according to the constitutional provisions of the Fifth Amendment, that no person, including the unborn child, could be deprived of the inalienable right to life, without duly convicting that person of a capital crime. It is unreasonable to suppose that the

Congresses of 1859 and 1874 which had, on federal territory, directly restricted, prohibited, and criminalized abortion would, during the very same period, indirectly have authorized abortion-on-demand in the Fourteenth Amendment, as Justice Blackmun insinuated in *Roe* v. *Wade*? As the great Chief Justice John Marshall was wont to say, no reasonable person anywhere could ever hope to maintain such a proposition.

So it is no surprise that the anti-abortion movement sometimes is perplexed that the so-called "right" to abortion-on-demand has enveloped the entire nation. We seem to be saying, "how can it *ever* be right to do wrong? If abortion is not wrong, *nothing* is wrong." But let us recall that in the 1850s, the anti-slavery movement was perplexed that the right to slavery, despite the inalienable right to liberty guaranteed in the Declaration, was advancing with the same inexorable drive throughout the vast new territories of the United States. That slavery spread rapidly with the doctrine of Manifest Destiny and the cotton gin, into the trans-Mississippi South and West, *before* the Civil War, is an indisputable fact of history. Historical research has confirmed Mr. Lincoln's controversial view in 1858 that slavery was *not* a dying, but a growing and profitable, institution. On all fronts slavery advanced, stronger in 1858 than in 1807, the year before the African slave trade was legally abolished. Can there be any more obvious analogy to the spread of the plague of abortion across the face of our nation after 1973?

But in 1860 the American people elected a new president, at the head of a new party, opposed in principle to slavery. And how did Mr. Lincoln and his new Republican party resist the extraordinary force of Supreme Court sponsorship of slavery? Invoking the precedents of Jefferson and Jackson, President Lincoln argued in his first inaugural speech of 1861, "if the policy of the [federal] government . . . is to be irrevocably fixed by decisions of the Supreme Court — the people will have ceased to be their own rulers." Following President Lincoln's lead, the Republican Congress, only one year later, moved against the Court and passed the congressional statute of 1862, which reversed the *Dred Scott* decision, overruled the Court, and prohibited the extension of slavery to all American territories. In 1863 came the Emancipation Proclamation; then, in 1865 and 1868 the Thirteenth and Fourteenth Amendments, all of which overthrew slavery and the *Dred Scott* Supreme Court forever.

Moved, as we are, by the *essential* principles of the Constitution, unequivocally enshrined in the Declaration of Independence, we call, in Mr. Lincoln's own word, for "the reversal" of *Roe* v. *Wade*. And, in this great work, we should be encouraged to know that President Andrew Jackson was, in fact, *wrong* when he said that the Courts have no more power over Congress than Congress has over the Courts. For the Constitution does bestow upon Congress much more authority over the Court than it gives to the Court over Congress. In Article III, section 2, Congress is given explicit constitutional power, if it chooses, to remove Supreme Court jurisdiction of all abortion cases. But nowhere in the four corners of the Constitution can anyone discover any explicit power of judicial review now exercised by the courts. Any thorough debate over Article III, section 2, will yield the unavoidable conclusion, fairly drawn from the Constitution itself, that if Congress wishes *even to eliminate lower* federal court jurisdiction in abortion cases, it can certainly do so without raising questions of due process, provided that it authorize state courts to review those same cases. For bold legislators who would reform the deep flaws in current Supreme Court practice the lesson is that a renegade Supreme Court can be constitutionally curbed by Congress. Congress need only truly desire to do so — just as the Congress of 1862 *did* so by overruling the Supreme Court's *Dred Scott* decision, and, by statute, prohibiting slavery in the territories.

It is clear, for example, that Congress could today, empowered by Article III, section 2, remove Supreme Court appellate jurisdiction (indeed, remove all federal court jurisdiction) of abortion cases. Congress could then pass a law defining human life as beginning from the very first moment of conception; further, that the inalienable right to life is the *paramount* right of those explicit human rights, enumerated in the Declaration of Independence, and in the Fifth and Fourteenth Amendments of the Constitution; moreover, that abortion should, to protect mother and child, be rigorously restricted. Finally, Congress could *require* that *all* states pass legislation to carry out the law of Congress, restricting public and private parties equally with respect to abortion. It would follow, all preceding court rulings like *Roe* v. *Wade* notwithstanding, that a congressional statute would necessarily become, according to the very words of the Constitution, the supreme law of the land.

Until that day, *Roe* v. *Wade* and *Casey* may, in some sense, be considered *legal* and binding on the parties in those particular cases; but still these decisions are, in the full sense of the word, illegitimate. In the light of logic, of the moral law, and of American history, *Roe* v. *Wade* and its illegitimate progeny are absurd; they come to nothing but "raw judicial power" — as sitting Supreme Court Justice Byron White declared in his lonely dissent of 1973.

Step by step, we are now led to consider the third of the co-equal constitutional branches of government — the presidency of the United States — the incumbent of which swears an irrevocable oath to "preserve, protect, and defend the Constitution of the United States of America." He, alone, who takes this *precise* constitutional oath, "registered in heaven," as Mr. Lincoln emphasized — he, alone, must interpret his duty to enforce the Constitution as he, sworn by a unique oath, is given to see it. The president might see clearly that he could encourage state legislatures to restrict abortion, just as he might use his moral leadership to insist that Congress do the same. When Congress acted to do so, the president would sign the statute into law and, in the case of state legislatures, publicly endorse their acts. Moreover, it is a constitutional truth that, under certain circumstances, the president has the full power to nullify directly, by constitutional executive authority, the action of the Court — which, in virtue of his constitutional duty, the president might be pledged to do. And if the president so acted, citing his sworn oath to "preserve, protect and defend the Constitution of the United States," especially in those grave matters of life and death when it may be urgent and necessary to oppose a spurious opinion of the Supreme Court, or any other court, it may be objected that there is *no* precedent for such extraordinary presidential action.

First, let it be said that the present slaughter of the innocents is an ultimate, extraordinary, and unprecedented threat of destruction to innocent human life in America, *and thus* to the foundation of the Constitution itself. Should all the fundamental laws *but one* be executed, even though that one, the inalienable right to life, be the basis of all the others?

Furthermore, there *is*, in fact, a clear and compelling precedent. During an equally grave national crisis of life and death in 1861, President Lincoln, acting alone, suspended "the privilege of the writ of *habeas corpus*," one of the most fundamental rights of Anglo-Saxon and American constitutional law. Immediately, the Supreme Court issued a writ to constrain the president. Confronted as he was with a writ of *habeas corpus*, issued against him in the Merryman case by the Chief Justice of the Supreme Court of the United States, what did Mr. Lincoln do? The president did not even acknowledge the writ of the Court. In fact, he ignored the Court — and its Chief Justice. The writ fell to the ground, without force. The suspension of *habeas corpus*, authorized by President Lincoln in order to save the Union, continued in effect, in virtue of the full constitutional authority of the Chief Executive of the United States. President Lincoln had ignored the writ of the Supreme Court, on the necessary and sufficient constitutional ground that the Chief Executive of the United States, given an ultimate threat to the life of the Union, must interpret *his* constitutional duty as *he*, the *president*, is given to understand it — *not* as the *Chief Justice* of the Supreme Court understands it.

Moreover, President Lincoln insisted he violated no law in suspending *habeas corpus*, and of course he did not; for the Constitution does provide for suspension of *habeas corpus*, under conditions of insurrection, and nowhere does it explicitly give that power to Congress alone. But to those who argued that he "might" have violated the Constitution, he did reply that his first obligation as president was to uphold his sworn oath to preserve the Union, without which there would be no Constitution, no laws to uphold, no further means to establish justice. "Are all the laws but one to go unexecuted," he queried, "and the government itself go to pieces, lest that one be violated?"

Assembled here at Philadelphia, twenty-three years after *Roe v. Wade*, in the very home of the Declaration of Independence, we cannot escape our history. In that time, thirty-five million abortions in America have destroyed thirty-five million babies. "I tremble for my country" when I hear, rising over Independence Hall, like thunder across the Delaware Valley, the echo of the words of Mr. Jefferson and Mr. Lincoln ringing in my ears. Is it truly to be supposed that, today, all the laws of the nation *are* to be executed, except the most fundamental one, the inalienable right to life, our birthright — the authority and security of which is the very basis of the American republic? Is it truly to be supposed that the annihilation of the child-in-the-womb is to go on and on and on, and that no constitutional power on earth, neither Court, nor Congress, nor president, nor even the people of the United States shall empower themselves to stop this holocaust? Surely no people upholding the Declaration of Independence, could, against all history and justice, sustain such a proposition.

What then are true patriots to do? How can we compromise with the abortion power? What will satisfy them? I answer, in Mr. Lincoln's nearly exact words at Cooper Union, one hundred thirty-six years ago (with but a substitution of one word): "Even though much provoked, let us do nothing through passion and ill temper". . . But still we ask, "what will satisfy them? . . . This, and only this, cease to call [abortion] *wrong*, and join them in calling it right. . . . Holding as they do that [abortion] is morally right, and socially elevating, they cannot cease to demand a full recognition of it, as a legal right, and a social blessing. . . . Nor can we justifiably withhold this, on any ground save our conviction that [abortion] is wrong. If [abortion] is right, all words, acts, laws, and Constitutions against it, are themselves wrong, and should be silenced and swept away. If [abortion] is right, we cannot justly object to its universality; if it is wrong, they cannot justly insist upon it. All they ask, we *could* readily grant, if we thought [abortion] right; all *we* ask, they could as readily grant, if they thought it wrong. Thinking it right, as they do, they are not to blame for desiring its full recognition, but, thinking it wrong, as we do, can we yield to them? Can we cast our votes with their view, and against our own? In view of our moral, social, and political responsibilities, can we do this? . . . If our sense of duty forbids this, then let us stand by our duty, fearlessly and effectively. . . LET US HAVE *FAITH* THAT RIGHT MAKES MIGHT, AND IN THAT *FAITH*, LET US, TO THE END, DARE TO DO OUR DUTY AS WE UNDERSTAND IT."

Chapter IV
Alan Keyes

Realizing Our Human Potential in the Public Square

Everything about the future of this nation, everything about it — whether it shall turn out for good or ill — depends precisely upon you. The decision of your heart, whether before or whether now or whether later, will in fact determine the fate of this country. America is in a desperate crisis today. And contrary to what some folks would like us to believe, it is not a budgetary crisis, it is not a monetary crisis, it is not an international crisis. It is not a crisis of who has what jobs and what they make. It is not a crisis of what families bring in what kind of an income. We continue to convince ourselves that these issues are the most important issues in the world. Now we have people trying to convince us that if you are poor, it is better that you should not even be born.

But in the span of my brief career as an ambassador to the United Nations representing the interests of the United States, I have seen some of the worst areas of poverty on the face of this earth. I have seen people living without shelter, without money, without food, and without adequate clothing. I have seen people living in places where the sewers were open and where flies flocked on the bodies of the elderly and children. Yet in the midst of those horrors of material oppression, I saw families — people living as husbands and wives and as parents and children. Family is not about what you have in your pocket, it is about what you have in your heart. Indeed the most important issue facing our country and the world is the decline of the family.

There is no degree of material poverty that can by itself wipe out that treasure of the heart — the family. Yet if we look around us, then we will see families that are dying. As the family dies, the nation dies with them. We are drowning in the sickness of our own lack of discipline and our own lack of a sense of responsibility. And where does it come from? What is the real nature of the crisis we are in?

The other day on cable television, there was an interesting trailer for a documentary on Home Box Office (HBO). The title of the documentary was "Without Pity." It was about those who are called *differently-abled* or *specially-abled*. In the past, they were called the disabled — people who have problems in their physical condition. It is about how numbers of these people have been able, in spite of their bodily problems, to overcome the obstacles and to lead lives of success and achievement that would be remarkable even in those of us blessed by God to be more physically whole. For all the expressed admiration of the producers of "Without Pity," I wonder if they realize what is the real lesson behind those who are endowed with this special challenge of physical deformities. It is not a lesson about our bodies. It is actually a lesson about the truth. Whatever the form or deformity of our bodies, there is in each and everyone one of us a potential determined not by that form, and not by any human perception of it, but rather by the absolute power and will of Almighty God. The truth that we can draw upon when we are faced with whatever material circumstances that might threaten to deform the real meaning of our humanity is not bound and not determined by our physical condition, circumstances, or sensual perception, but rather by that power which has made us, which transcends those circumstances, and which can lift us above them. On the one hand, how can the producers of HBO (past promoters of the abortion doctrine and the pro-choice movement) purport to be people who understand that the human essence and the human potential is not determined by the form or deformity of our physical selves? And at the same time that they purport the fact that a mother — or anyone of us — has the right to reach into the womb and rip out and destroy the human fetus on account of the physical form or deformity of that life? If we are supposed to see the human worth and human potential of the specially-abled in the world, then we must realize the reality of their human essence and the their right to be respected even if those specially-abled are in the womb.

The pro-abortion and pro-choice folks pretend to be compassionate. What is the heart of their compassion? For them, the word "compassion" can be readily applied at a national AIDS benefit or in a Hollywood movie to arouse in us a sense of pity for the poor, the undesirable, the hungry, or the disabled. The real heart of compassion is understood when we have realized the truth of our humanity; that is, when we strive to look upon it not with the deformed eye of the pro-choice folks, but rather with the true eye of Almighty God. In that eye of God, the truth is clear.

Recently I read a *New York Times* article written by a pro-abortion advocate about how the pro-abortion side is finally beginning to understand the true meaning of what it means to be human. It is further proof that they have lost the argument about human life. Indeed, no well-researched person can accept the foolish notion that we are not dealing with our humanity in the womb. This author of the article wrote about how the pro-choice movement has to show some maturity and realize that the act of conception is something special and something sacred. And then she wrote these words, "Human life is sacred, but there are times when one life is more sacred than another." As I read those words, I knew the truth was out. The whole pro-choice movement (not just the hardcore pro-abortion organizations) rests on the principle that some of us are worth more than others and that some of us have an intrinsic worth that gives us the right to look upon the labor, the bodies, and the rights of others as if they were no more important than a roach to be stamped out by our own will. This central argument of the pro-choice movement is a lie that is meant to destroy what this nation was founded to refute.

This argument did not begin in the guns and the arms of the guards enforcing the horrors at Auschwitz. It did not begin in the mind of Adolph Hitler. It did not begin in the speeches that corrupted the heart of his German compatriots. It did not begin in 1945. Those horrors which have deformed our century and which I believe shall make it a century that, should the human spirit survive it, we will look back in shame upon this century of degradation, I believe that those horrors began with this very thought — the idea that some of us are intrinsically worth more than others.

This is not just a rejection of the founding ethical principle of our Christian faith and our Catholic heart. It is also a rejection of the founding principle of our nation on which its very existence and the existence of all the liberties of its citizens rests. All men are created equal. We are equal not in talents, not in education, not in money, not in strength, not in power, not in beauty, not in form or deformity, but equal rather in the moral truth of our existence. We share in the spark of God's divinity. We share in the fire of God which must be respected by every human will, by every human person, whatever the circumstances.

The pro-abortion movement represents the rejection of this truth. This rejection is not only a cause, but it is a manifestation of the spirit of our times. And why do I call your attention to this spirit? Is it to dispirit you? No. On any given day of the week you look at what is going on in this country and I would not blame you for getting discouraged. But I believe that things look better than they are. And that is when you are really in trouble. If we were in the midst of a great physical calamity, or if the threat were international in scope, or if the economy were crumbling and the streets were filled with the groans of the starving, I have a feeling that spiritual renewal would be easier in America. As you know, just as there are a few atheists in the fox hole, so there are a few atheists in the deep trenches of human existence.

We are a nation almost ready to pride ourselves that we stand at the pinnacle of human achievement with our adversaries at our feet. The hardest things we have to achieve are whether our growth rate will be 2.6 or 3.7 percent. These trivialities will not sustain us. It does not matter whether the growth rate is 2.6, 3.7, 4.5, or 6.0. If that principle of horror and evil in this century — that some of us are intrinsically worth more than others — continues and permanently overtakes the conscience and consciousness of this land, then that will be a harbinger, not only for this nation, but for the world. If this idea continues, then we should fear for our children and their children and the twentieth century will become a dress rehearsal of evil to come. The way to turn back this principle of evil in this nation is to be dedicated to the principle of hope.

I believe deeply that this is the challenge we are facing in America. It is actually easier than one might think to dwell upon all the terrible things that face this country. It is becoming easier and easier for us to understand the truth of our spiritual poverty, and to begin to appreciate the practical horrors of family destruction, of teenage crime and violence, of deteriorating scholarship, and of every kind of material deformity that are natural effects of our moral decay. We can begin to see it. In fact, what may be harder to see is the real source of hope in the midst of our spiritual poverty. If there is hope in America, that hope is you.

I believe that our principles of unity as Americans far outweigh our principles of difference. We can stand a common ground of moral concern and discover not only our common creed as Christians but our common creed as Americans overcoming all the differences of faith and race and background. For all that truth, I cannot help but feel that our Catholic heritage gives us a special place; it gives us a special challenge in America today. Do you remember the primary season on the Republican side? Do you think it was an accident that the three most outspoken advocates of the unvarnished truth about the need to stand and bare witness to the pro-life cause were Catholic Christians? It was no accident. We should feel good about this fact. If we do not live up to the promise of this gift of our Faith, we will be remembered as the guy "weeping and gnashing his teeth" from the parable in the Gospels.

Our heritage cannot be a source of baseless human pride. It must be rather what it is supposed to be, that which inspires us to greater love of Jesus Christ and God His Father. In this way, everyday we grow in greater love and greater willingness to do, whatever the cost of God's will. In America today, I think this means we have to bear witness to things nobody wants to hear about much anymore; that is, to the real consequences of love. People talk about it so much. But we — as Catholic Christians — talk about love today like it was a passion, like it was a feeling, because what we are talking about is the love of Christ.

Christ's love is a moral condition. It is a moral truth. It is a willingness to take all the passion, all the sentiment, and all the feeling, and martial it behind one dedication to the Word and will of God Almighty. This is true love. This love is what will bring this nation back to decency. We need to hear this which the Holy Father has been trying to tell us — that man does not live on bread alone. You can do all you want out there, saving the bodies of the poor, ministering to the needs of the hungry in a physical sense. If in order to do so you sign on to perpetuate doctrines that reduce human beings to their bodies and their physical needs, then you have invited them to do that which Christ said we should never do, which is to gain the world at the cost of our living soul and the living truth of our spiritual lives.

There is no compassion in the welfare that destroys moral discipline. There is no compassion in the public policy programs that invite people to abandon their moral hearts in order to live out their material needs. If we allow ourselves as a Church, as a people, and as individuals to be put in service of that erroneous understanding of compassion, then we shall join with those who are using and abusing the true meaning of compassion in order to lead this nation to perdition. We need to examine our lives at this most critical time for our nation and ask ourselves if we are meeting the challenge of our Faith and the challenge of our crucified Savior, which is to take up His cross and to follow Him — even to those lonely places where no one will understand, where no one will join with us, and where no one will ask how we could seem to be so contrary to the spirit of our times. We must remember that it is not for the spirit of our times that we live, but for the Holy Spirit which comes to us from Him who transcends time and Who continually speaks to us with words of comfort and peace.

If we are true to Christ's love, we will be true to our best vocation and to ourselves. We shall win ourselves to the truth and we shall win our nation to salvation. In the process, we shall live out the words of that old song: "This little light of mine, I'm gonna let it shine. . . ." The light will not be so small as you think, because the light that is supposed to shine from us has been, by the grace of God, put in a place where it can be amplified. And through the restoration of our nation's moral will and identity, it shall be a light that calls the world to light. This light is the salvation we can win through Jesus Christ. May God bless you and love you.

Chapter V
Anne Ryder

"Hope to Tell" in the Media

One of my favorite sayings is that coincidence is God's way of creating a miracle anonymously. With God's grace and blessing, I believe this saying applies to me in many instances in my life. In this short essay, I want to relay to you some of my experiences of "coincidence" as a local news anchor at Channel 13 (WTHR) in Indianapolis.

As part of my job as co-anchor of the nightly news, I do a series entitled "Hope to Tell: Stories of Hope and Faith." Each piece is a story of hope, faith, and resilience of the human spirit in the world. Unfortunately, you rarely see this type of story on mainstream newscasts. You certainly do not see it very often on national network news.

The "Hope to Tell" project was born, as most good projects are, through prayer. Some background first. Even though I have worked very hard to get where I am today, I have been lucky. Five years ago, I was the consumer reporter in the twenty-fourth largest market station in the country, anchoring the five, six, and eleven o'clock news. Yet, most of our material consisted of drive-by shootings, gangs, and what Roseanne Barr was up to. I was frustrated because all the stories we were doing were on violence and people's "dirty laundry." I was longing for more balance in our news coverage. I asked myself, why can't the news be more balanced? Why can't we tell our viewers about the people who come into our lives and give us verbal bouquets of sunshine?

We meet people like this everyday. You see something in their eyes. You may be having a horrible day when someone, perhaps a perfect stranger, makes your day. This is real news. More times than not, I find that the light in their eyes has to do with their faith. I thought, "Why can't there be some mechanism for bringing that onto the news on a regular basis so that when people turn on the news, they get something that makes them feel good, instead of something that makes them feel bad?"

My first opportunity to clearly report on a story of faith came when the pope arrived in Denver for World Youth Day in August 1993. My producers thought that I would be good for the assignment since I was a recent convert to Catholicism. I was thrilled to be able to go to Denver. For those of you who were there, you know that the Holy Spirit was present. It was everywhere. There was something magic about that gathering. People were calling into the station saying it was coming through in my reporting. The audience response was so positive, my station management started to believe in the power of these stories.

After the success of our coverage in Denver, I approached my general manager (a Catholic) and asked him about the prospect of covering a pilgrimage to Medjugorje. This is the village in Bosnia where many people believe the Virgin Mary appears to local children. Even though it was during the height of the Bosnian war, there were groups from Indiana going on a regular basis. I thought that this story would be a great witness to the faith — of grandmothers, grandfathers, fathers, mothers, children — and deserved to be covered. It's news, by anybody's standard. In fact, the State Department was warning groups not to go, and yet they did. When I pitched the story to my general manager, he loved it, as a means of kicking off an ongoing news feature called "Hope to Tell." What a way to begin!

A few days before we were scheduled to leave, we found out that there was a problem with something called the "carnet." A carnet, basically, is international insurance — if your equipment gets confiscated, you will get it back through diplomatic channels. It is important to news crews to have this; in our case, we were traveling with $250,000 worth of equipment. We discovered the former Yugoslavia is one of the very few places on earth that does not honor a carnet. The new president of the company voiced concerns about sending a crew and the equipment into a war zone without protection. The trip was in jeopardy. My general manager said he would take personal responsibility for our well-being and for the equipment. With many prayers, my photographer and I left for Bosnia.

What a journey. Yet after a few days on the ground, I found myself confused and anxious as to how I was going to tell this story. On one hand, I witnessed very quiet, beautiful, and peaceful praying. I felt a great sense of peace in the village. On the other hand, I saw people running around saying they were experiencing "miracles" like rosaries turning into gold and seeing the sun spin in the sky. I'm not saying miracles don't happen in Medjugorje. Many credible people say they do. It's just that I didn't experience anything dramatic or "miraculous." I was frustrated by this.

Since this time, I have learned how God communicates with me. God gets me on my knees, frustrated by my attempts to control, and then He comes through to me and communicates with me. My frustration in this case was compounded because I was afraid some of these pious people would look crazy, talking about the sun spinning.

My frustration mounted as I entered the room where the apparitions have been taking place. Again, I expected to "feel" something. I honestly felt more of the Holy Spirit when I was in Denver than I did in Bosnia. In the room, I saw people all around me who obviously felt something. I thought "what's wrong with me?" I said to myself, "Why can't I feel it?" My husband, who had gone with me on the trip, was feeling the same sense of frustration I was.

When I got out of the apparition room, I was greeted by an Irish nun who took both my hands in hers and she said, "I have been watching you all week long." She said that she taught at an abbey in Ireland and that she was taking pictures of me so she could show her students that someone could have a rosary in one hand and a microphone in the other. I confided in her my frustration, and the fact that I wasn't getting any "miracles." She told me that I was in Medjugorje to work and that I was doing "Mary's work." She told me not to worry about whether or not I was feeling any miracles and to concentrate on attending to my work. She said that everything else would take care of itself. She was right. It gave me focus and perspective.

Later, my husband and I ran into a priest from Grand Rapids, Michigan, who was leading a group there. He referred us to 1 Kings 19, in which Elijah is looking for God. He looks for God in the earthquake, in the fire, and in the wind. But he doesn't find God in any of those things. Then he goes into a cave, and it is there that God comes to him in a whisper. I believe God whispers to most of us. The most important thing is for us to listen, to be still enough to hear God's whisper. My miracle was God whispering to me to go to Medjugorje and to have the chance to communicate the story as a newscaster. After that, I found great peace in the journey.

When I came back and sat down to write this story, I felt this tremendous sense of peace. I asked God for help in writing the story because I knew that He had to be the vehicle. I had to get out of the way of it. The documentary was a tremendous success. We dubbed the tape into all different kinds of VHS formats. It was written up in a magazine and we got tape orders from all over the world, including Ireland, Great Britain, Germany, Guam, and Haiti. It was incredible. We received very little negative commentary, considering what a spiritual story it was, unlike anything we had ever aired on our newscast.

One woman I featured in the story became a spiritual friend. Marilyn Wethington had learned that she had ovarian cancer about a year before making this trip. She hated airplanes and had no intention of going to Medjugorje, despite prodding by her sister, Laurel. But prior to the trip, Marilyn was out on a Greenwood, Indiana, golf course. She pulled out her golf ball and heard something clink. She bent down and picked up a tiny medal from the grass. It was a Medjugorje medal, with the unmistakable markings of the village and the Virgin Mary. Marilyn's sister assured her she had not put it in her golf bag. Marilyn considered it a sign from God and got the last seat on the airplane.

It was such a joy to watch Marilyn in Medjugorje. I watched this brave woman who was fighting cancer realize, for the first time, what the Lord's Prayer really means. Especially "thy will be done." Like me, Marilyn learned to relinquish control. A year later she died, but her story and her faith touched thousands of people through the documentary.

My second "major" story of "Hope to Tell" was the story of Air Force Captain Scott O'Grady. He was the young pilot who spent six harrowing days in Bosnia after Serbs shot his F-16 out of the sky. After his dramatic and triumphant rescue, I was touched by the first words out of his mouth: "If it wasn't for my love for God and God's love for me, I wouldn't be here right now and I know that in my heart." I saw the light in his eyes and thought, there's more to this story than we are getting.

Scott initially did just two interviews, one with Larry King of CNN and the other with Jane Pauley of NBC. During the Pauley interview, O'Grady mentioned that he had heard of a place called Medjugorje, near where he was shot down. He said a friend once told him people saw miracles there but he never believed it, until now. He said, while on the ground some eighty miles away, he "saw something." I leaned forward to hear what he saw, but Jane Pauley never asked! I began calling the Pentagon.

I called so often, trying to track down an interview with Scott, that a woman there finally told me that even Barbara Walters could not get an interview; why did an Indianapolis reporter think Scott would speak to her? I said I wanted to ask him about his spiritual experience while on the ground. Twenty minutes later, Scott O'Grady called me back.

He proceeded to tell me an amazing story that had not been told. On his third day on the ground in Bosnia, he said he was praying to everybody he could think of — from God the Father, to Jesus, to the Holy Spirit, and even to his deceased aunt. O'Grady said he thought about the village of Medjugorje, and sent up a prayer to the Virgin Mary. To this day, Scott has a very difficult time articulating what happened next. He says there are no words in English to adequately explain it. But he says when he prayed to the Virgin Mary, he could see her as a shimmering image, but that the image came through a feeling, a feeling more important than the image. He said it was the most intense and powerful feeling of love that he has ever felt, like warm arms wrapped around him. He says it was a thousand times stronger than any feeling of love he has felt on earth. He says he knew it was God, and that no matter what happened, whether he lived or died, he was with God. He says it sustained him through his six-day ordeal.

Scott O'Grady says after his rescue, he was on such a spiritual high that when it ebbed two weeks later, he felt guilty, feeling that his intense level of prayer had fallen off. He said a priest helped him realize that God is always as close as his next prayer, and that God was there for him when he needed it, even if the intensity of feeling had waned.

No other reporter had asked Scott O'Grady about his spiritual experience. He details it in his book *Return with Honor*. Scott O'Grady has become a good friend. I consider his friendship another blessing from God.

The third in what I call the "Hope to Tell" trilogy has to do with Mother Teresa. In January 1996, I wrote Mother Teresa a letter, telling her about "Hope to Tell." She wrote me back, telling me she does not do television interviews, but inviting me to come to Calcutta and "share in our works of love." I knew in advance that Mother Teresa has turned down nearly every television journalist, from Dan Rather to Barbara Walters. But I was thrilled just to get an invitation to come and work in her homes for the poor, even without cameras allowed inside.

I convinced our general manager to send two photographers with me to Calcutta, even if we had to tell the story in a first-person nontraditional way. In a remarkable demonstration of faith in "Hope to Tell," the general manager approved the $20,000 trip, with no guarantee of a story.

I wondered to myself whether I was going for personal or professional reasons — all I knew is I was going to go, whether the station sent me or I just went on my own. I am grateful that, in the end, I had the support of my station. But I did not tell my station what I learned shortly before making the journey. Two days before I had to get the final medical shots, I found out that after years and years of trying and praying, I was pregnant with my first child. It was a high-risk pregnancy, made even higher by the prospect of traveling ten thousand miles into an area wracked by disease.

My husband and I consulted three doctors. They said yes, it was a risk to go, and yes, there are shots for protection. My husband and I prayed about it intensely. Should I make the journey? Why would God allow me to get pregnant now? The moral of this story is be careful what you pray for because I was praying for

God's will on the Mother Teresa story and also on a baby. I got both at once!

God's timing seemed to leave something to be desired. But when I prayed to Him, I felt, in the silence of prayer, four words: "Do you trust me?" I know now that God's timing was perfect. I shared the trip of a lifetime with my unborn child.

Physically the journey the was very, very tough. It was about one hundred five degrees in Calcutta. I worked in Mother Teresa's home for the mentally ill the first day. One of the things Mother Teresa says is that you have to get out of your "comfort zone" in order to have your heart touched. I learned that within five minutes. The volunteers were bathing the women's bodies and the women looked like something out of the holocaust. Their skin was barely on their bones. Most of the women were in a crouched position, so malnourished they couldn't stand up. I was out of my comfort zone all right.

Someone put a rag and a piece of soap in my hands and I began helping to bathe the women. But on my second attempt, the woman shrieked when I put water on her. I didn't know what to do. We didn't speak the same language. I tried again to soap her body. She screamed again and I backed off. Yet I knew she wanted a bath. So, finally, I put down the sponge and the soap and I just put my hands on her back. I rubbed her back very gently for about ten minutes. The other volunteers were bathing three and four women in the time it took me to rub the back of this one. Finally she let me bathe her entire body. It took a long time. I dried her off and I put a new dress on her. She looked up at me with so much love in her eyes — it must be like a child looks up at a parent sometimes — and I immediately knew what I had read in all the books about Mother Teresa. She says it's not how much you do that matters, but how much love with which you do it. I finally understood that lesson, firsthand.

I had tried to empty myself spiritually before I went to Calcutta. I thought I can't go as a typical journalist, full of control, aggressive, and demanding. I knew I'd have to empty myself spiritually to communicate this story. On my third day, I met with Sister Priscilla, who is Mother Teresa's right-hand person. I was told she is not fond of the media. By my third day, Sister Priscilla was mighty curious about me because I had not made any attempt to try to pressure anybody into an interview. My photographers had kept their distance, getting street shots of Calcutta. I had a remarkable ten-minute conversation with Sister Priscilla. She asked me why I was there. I told her I wanted to share the story of love and care in whatever way I was permitted to do so. We spoke about negative news and the project "Hope to Tell." Sister Priscilla softened a bit, and asked me if I had seen their home for people with leprosy. I said no, not yet. She said, "Go there tomorrow. Take your crew." Then she proceeded to give me permission to photograph each of the five homes.

On our last day, we interviewed Mother Teresa. I could not believe it. We became the first American crew in twelve years to get that kind of access. I felt the hand of God touch this project. And speaking of blessings, on our last day, during my interview with Mother Teresa, she blessed my unborn baby. I was just a few months pregnant. She put her hands on my belly and said, "Mary, Mother of Jesus, just as you protected the baby Jesus in your womb, please protect this baby." Tears filled my eyes. I now know why God had the timing He did. What a lucky baby.

We have sold thirteen hundred copies of the documentary we produced, called "In the Arms of Mother Teresa." Again, we've had requests from all over the country. The station is donating all proceeds to the Missionaries of Charity. An Indianapolis drug manufacturer, on seeing the documentary, sent enough antibiotics to Mother Teresa's leprosy center to treat five thousand lepers.

I don't know where God will lead "Hope to Tell" next, but I do know He walks beside it, just as He walks with each of us. We have only to listen, in the silence of our hearts, to hear His whisper.

Chapter VI
Reverend Michael Scanlan, T.O.R.

Hope in the Public Square

Hope is the essential virtue for those who labor in the public square, working within our political system to bring about the changes this country so desperately needs. But in the midst of our work we can easily get caught up in all sorts of attacks and confusion, spiritual warfare, and political strategizing, and forget that our hope is in Christ Jesus and in his Church.

As we read in the First Letter of Peter, we must "Always be ready to give an explanation to anyone who asks you for a reason for your hope" (1 Peter 3:15). God is always our hope. We have to stand as men and women who believe that we have a future, a hope, and even a triumph, not because of what man does, but because of what God does within each of us. God doesn't get tired. God isn't defeated by the latest poll. God is new every morning, and he calls us to proclaim that newness and hope to whomever we serve. But this "new evangelization," as Pope John Paul II calls it, has to begin with us renewing ourselves individually and with the Church renewing herself. The Holy Father says we do this by being charmed by Jesus Christ; that is, by falling in love with Him. If we fall in love with Him and remain in love with Him, we will be empowered. We can then go out and introduce others to Jesus Christ our Lord, our Master, our Friend, our Redeemer, our Savior. He, indeed, is the hope of the world.

His hope can sustain us, no matter how hard things get, how much our work costs us personally. One of the greatest experiences of hope I have had in my life happened when I visited Auschwitz, Poland. It was an unusual place to find hope, a place so inexorably linked with the horror of the degradation of man. But to prepare for the pilgrimage I was leading, I had read three books on the life of St. Maximilian Kolbe, a man whose hope and faith transcended even the horror of Auschwitz.

As I walked into the camp, I realized that Maximilian Kolbe

had probably worn the exact same type of Franciscan habit that I was wearing. As we walked by cell after cell, we saw the toys of little children, the hair shaved from the heads of the people who'd been gassed, the piles of teeth pulled from the prisoners' mouths in a search for gold. We saw the people's medals and prayer books and realized how much they'd been stripped. We glimpsed the agony of these people who existed for only weeks before they were killed.

Maximilian had kept praying through all these circumstances. He was full of hope and communicated that hope to others. He was patient, seeking to help others, giving away his food, taking the hardest jobs, concentrating constantly on other people, and assuring them that yes, they may die, but they would not be conquered. They would conquer the Nazis, hunger, and death, because the Immaculata was with them.

In August 1941, an inmate escaped from Kolbe's barrack. The guards made all the prisoners stand outside in the hot sun while they searched for the escapee. Finally, the commandant declared that ten from that barrack would be starved to death as punishment for the escape of the one. He went through the ranks, picking one, then another. As the ten were pulled forward, one man, Sergeant Francis Gajowniczek, cried out, "Oh, my wife and my children! What will happen to them?" Suddenly, Maximilian moved from his place in line, walked up to the commandant, kissed his hand, and asked to die in Francis Gajowniczek's place. The commandant agreed.

Kolbe and the others were stripped and thrown into a bunker to slowly starve to death. But, as the orderlies testified later, Maximilian gathered the group together and talked about God's love and led them in prayer and song, assuring them of their conquest, their victory. One by one they died and were dragged out of the bunker by an orderly, until finally there were only three men left. On August 14, the orderly found that only one man was alive, his face aglow, smiling with victory. They injected Maximilian with poison, and he went home to glory.

This is indeed a horrible story, but through it all Maximilian Kolbe never lost the truth that God loved him. When I came out of

Auschwitz, I knew there was nothing in this life that could separate us from the love of Christ Jesus. I knew that God had poured the Holy Spirit out in our hearts. I knew there was nothing that could happen in this world that could take away our hope, if we clung to the Lord and the Church.

Like Maximilian, we in this Catholic Campaign for America have to be men and women of hope, who believe in the triumph of the Lord, who believe that the gates of hell will not prevail against the Church. We who believe in this triumph over evil must stand ready to give an explanation of our hope. Even in times of confusion and difficulty, we must witness to this hope.

My friend Rose Totino was a great witness of hope. She launched NET, the National Evangelization Teams that travel the country witnessing to high school students. She was a great Catholic and a great evangelizer. When she was on her deathbed, her children called and asked me to pray for her. I did. They called again and told me Rose was in a coma. They thought it was all over.

A few hours later she came out of the coma, and said, "It is so bright here." When the children asked where she was, Rose said she didn't know but that "everything is so bright." They asked if Jesus was there. She said, "Yes, but he's farther down. I'm going to him." Then she began repeating, "It is worth it . . . everything is so worth it. Eye has not seen, ear has not heard, nor has it entered into the heart of man to experience the wonders God has in store for his people!" In the end, she smiled, and said to her family, "Next one up, bring my sunglasses."

This woman, who was eighty-some years old, was truly a woman of hope and gave so much hope to her children. No matter what happens to us on this earth, we are going to have a great family reunion in heaven. No matter what happens to us, there is glory in heaven. No matter what happens in our lives, Jesus wants us at the banquet table. Jesus has prepared a place for us, and he has poured hope into our hearts through the Holy Spirit. Touch it! Know it! Live it! And be prepared to give an explanation of that hope to everyone.

I want to tell you another story of hope. It's about one of our students. She was a top student. She had a National Institute of

Health fellowship. She was a campus ministry leader and a leader of Magnificat Household, her small share group. In her senior year, in the midst of all these successes, she was diagnosed with terminal cancer. Though the doctors tried every kind of remedy, she deteriorated quickly. I talked to her a number of times over the year, and soon it was clear that she wasn't coming back to the University.

She had one motto — which all the students knew — "Take delight in the Lord, and he will give you your heart's desire." The week before she died, the Lord appeared to her in her hospital room. She asked him for one more week, because she still hadn't finished witnessing to her old high school classmates. The Lord gave her permission, so as they came to say good-bye, she told them about the joy of being Christian and Catholic, about the Lord Jesus who was the joy of her life. She told them she was looking forward to going home with the Lord. When she finished, she passed on to the Lord.

What all these stories tell us is that we, too, must be witnesses of God's hope in whatever circumstances we find ourselves. As we read in Romans, we must boast of our hope for the glory of God: "We know that affliction makes for endurance, and endurance for tested virtue, and tested virtue for hope. And this hope will not leave us disappointed, because the love of God has been poured out in our hearts through the Holy Spirit" (Romans 5:2-5).

The stories also tell us that we have to be witnesses of the gift of the Catholic Church herself. We must rejoice in the "splendor of the Church" as it's called by Cardinal Henri de Lubac. He proclaims the need for men and women to fall in love with the beauty of the house of God — the Church, which has stolen their hearts; she is their spiritual native country.

Today, there is a lot of confusion, controversy, and bad news in the Church and in the world. But that's not where our hope lies. Our hope is in Christ Jesus, through whom we are more than conquerors. Let us go forth as conquerors and give hope to the world and to one another.

Chapter VII
Senator Rick Santorum

Raising Our Consciences on Partial-Birth Abortion

As a Catholic, I have tried my best to fulfill what I identify as two imperatives of my Faith: private devotion and public witness. Both are very important to me, both help to sustain me and I, in turn, am sustained and moved by others' commitment to these very same imperatives. My role in the Senate, has, in several ways, both challenged and affirmed my identity as a Catholic and a Christian. The most obvious example of this challenge and reaffirmation is seen through the prism of the abortion debate, particularly the partial-abortion debate. But I will discuss that in a few minutes. First, I would like to talk a little about the more personal part of my Faith.

Because there is an important battle being waged in our country — of thought, of values, and of standards — the support and prayers from people of faith mean a tremendous amount to me. It is so heartening to know so many people are supporting you, praying for you, holding you up. It is a tremendous motivation and comfort. That most personal part of our Faith — private prayer — can help to accomplish great things in public. So that even those who do not stand on the Senate floor, or on the House floor, or in front of a large group speaking, or in front of that television camera, should remember that your prayers uphold many, many of us in public life.

In fact, in the Senate, there are anywhere from six to ten members that meet every Thursday at noon, right off the Senate floor, for Bible study. It is a small, bipartisan Bible study in which I feel privileged to participate every week. It is conducted by the chaplain of the Senate. We discuss a variety of concerns and issues, including the tremendous motivation we feel from the support we receive on issues such as partial-birth abortion. Clearly, I am not the only one who feels this support; many of us are upheld and strengthened by it. We understand the grassroots movements that are growing in this country — movements which seek to reestablish a moral foothold, to reestablish values and standards. That is why it is so important for a grassroots organization like the Catholic Campaign for America to be engaged in the public debate, to survive, and to continue to gather strength in this difficult time of moral relativism that continues to have momentum in our culture.

Which brings me to the more public part of my Faith. As I said, the best example I can give you of a witness to my Faith and "the Faith of our fathers" is on the issue of abortion. When I say public witness, I mean, in the very American context of deriving certain public principles of my Faith and of developing policies that adequately reflect those principles so that there is some animating force to my public service, rather than a rote commitment to certain procedural norms.

My thinking on the issue of abortion has matured and developed because of the kinds of people who participate in and support the Catholic Campaign for America. I have been challenged and inspired by their own willingness to stand up on very difficult issues such as abortion. It is one of those issues that people do not like to talk about; an issue that is controversial; an issue that is emotional. But I have taken a stand of this issue and I am glad to be identified with it in the public square.

I admit to you that in the six years that I have been in the House and Senate I have rarely stood on the floor and said, prior to this issue, the word "abortion." I do not know whether it was deliberate or not, but I never did. I can tell you, however, that I felt absolutely and overwhelmingly compelled to talk about the issue of partial-birth abortion. I talked about this issue on the floor of the Senate and talked about it very candidly. Why? This issue moved me as no other has. I believe it to be emblematic of what is wrong with our culture. When the Senate first voted on partial-birth abortion, I sat there on the floor listening to Bob Smith and Barbara Boxer debate this issue. I reflected back to when I was a child. This conversation could never have taken place on the floor of the Senate. This issue would never have been debated *anywhere* in this country, not even in Berkeley or Harvard. I simply cannot imagine this conversation taking place thirty years ago, simply because the common consensus against such a procedure would have precluded the need for any such "debate." And there we were on the floor of the United States Senate and we had a close vote. It was a close vote. Fifty-four Senators stood up and said that partial-birth abortion was wrong. Most of them voted as they did because they thought this was an issue where a line could be drawn and should be drawn.

For me, partial-birth abortion was certainly an issue where I decided that I can no longer stay silent. While it may not be politically popular to do that and it may not be in my long-term political interest, there are things that are more important. After the bill was passed, though, I knew that President Clinton would not sign it. It is simply not in his character to do that. I could not let this issue percolate along and the media to continue to bury it, and allow many people to remain uninformed about it. I knew that if I were to remain silent, I would be in complicity with those who supported this gruesome procedure. And so I decided to do something about it. I decided that here, in this most critical debate, my deeply held beliefs were called forth to public witness.

I called the Catholic Campaign for America and other leaders and asked them to come together and discuss the issue. And they did. We started an organization called the "Child Protection Fund." Some terrific people became involved and took a leadership role, including Admiral Jim Watkins (former Secretary of Energy), and Mary Ellen Bork. Our own Bill Donahue, who is from Pittsburgh and who has been a dear friend, became an active part of this organization. We worked very hard to develop ideas about how to effectively communicate the truth about this issue. Pollsters told us that if the public actually knew what the procedure was, a very large percentage of them would oppose it — which, of course, was comforting. What was not comforting is that there was still people who did not oppose it.

We designated an educational piece that would appeal to people's basic reason and most humane instincts regardless of their faith and views. It simply described what a partial-birth abortion was and how it was done. We used common language of facts to teach common knowledge of what is right and wrong that is written on each human heart — the language of natural law. We were energized by the fact that if we educated the public about the horrors of partial-birth abortions — of the horror of late-term abortions of healthy viable babies — then we might have an opportunity to pull off a miracle: change the twelve votes in the Senate needed for an override the President's veto. Twelve votes is a lot of votes in the United States Senate. But I knew that we needed to do something dramatic. And so a group of senators, including me, Senator Dewine, Senator Abraham, and Senator Coats became the main organizers. The speaker of the House, Newt Gingrich, was also tremendously helpful in aiding this organization.

We decided to produce a series of television advertisements which would educate voters about the stark reality of partial-birth abortion and air them before the Senate vote to override the President's veto. We ran the ads in twenty-six states. We raised money for these ads simply by picking up the phone and calling other people who cared about protecting the unborn. So that is the story of how people's private faith can animate their public role in a legitimate and fruitful way.

Many abortion proponents say that there are only a few hundred partial-birth abortions per year. Of course, this is not true. In a recent article, a reporter for the Bergen County Record in New Jersey said that there are fifteen hundred abortions in New Jersey alone performed every year. But even if it was one child, what does it say about us if we were to allow such an indefensible act to be legally sanctioned? What would it reveal about us if we could stand here and let a beautiful, viable, healthy baby be delivered and killed? In our country we have many people, particularly in public life, who can manipulate language so that it obscures the truth — especially when that truth is very unpalatable. But ultimately, I believe that we are a country and a civilization who stands for what we do, not what we say.

If we allow this tragedy of partial-birth abortions to continue and if we don't take a stand here, then I think we, as a people, could be defined for a long time by our abandonment of the unborn to this brutality. We cannot let this happen on our watch. We cannot have the next generation look at us and ask, "Why didn't you do all you could to stop this?" You will be thankful you allowed your private faith to animate an urgently needed public witness. Thank you and God bless you.

Postscript: On September 26, 1996, the vote for an override of President Clinton's veto of the partial-birth abortion ban fell short of the required two-thirds majority by nine votes.

Chapter VIII
Joseph A. Stibora

Evangelizing in an Increasingly Secular Society

There has been a heated debate among our Catholic political theorists in the last couple of generations, a debate which has had significant ramifications in both the Church and in American politics. The principal topic of contention concerns the relationship between the American political order and the Catholic character of its citizens. It is, in other words, a contemporary version of the ancient debate about the relationship between church and state. Today, Catholic political thinkers (and the Catholic laity in general) can be divided into three groups, if we consider the approaches they take to our "increasingly secular society."

That we are in an oppressively secular society, I think, will not be denied by too many people here today. "*Sanctificetur nomen tuum,*" we are *allowed* to say, but generally not in public, where we are apt to get sued, or have our funding taken away (a regular concern among academicians). The holy name of God is generally barred from civil discourse, replaced by the language of the physical and social sciences both lacking in true *scientia*. Man has overcome God, and Calculus has overcome man; the Marshallian supply-and-demand cross has replaced that of Christ, and the only invisible providence recognized is that of the almighty "market mechanism."

Catholics' responses

Though the utter degeneration of our American state makes us recall the old Catholic criticisms laid at the feet of liberalism by the likes of Popes Pius IX and Leo XIII (just as we recently recalled in *Centesimus Annus* the criticisms Leo laid at the feet of Communism), the fact that we are political beings by nature forces us to confront the threat of the barbarians as they sack and pillage our homeland. But how to confront those forces? In general, I would submit that there are three responses which have been proposed and have been adopted by the faithful.

The first response I hesitantly call the "Noble Lie." A couple of years ago, a devout Catholic gave a speech in honor of Constitution Day. Part of his thesis was: "The Declaration speaks of the laws of nature and nature's God; what could be more Catholic than natural law?; therefore, America could be a great place for Catholics." That speech begs the careful listener to ask, if only implicitly, whether the American founders were thinking in anything approaching Thomistic or even generally Catholic terms. For the sake of the necessary limitations to the city, Socrates tells his interlocutors in the original noble lie, citizens need to be told that they are different from noncitizens. What this story hides from the citizens is that, as men, they are the same as foreigners. Neither Jew nor Gentile, neither Greek nor Roman. For Catholics to be fully American, we need to hear and believe that we are just the same as non-Catholics, even non-Christians, not different. Even St. Thomas, perhaps, needs to be christened a Whig.

The second response to the contemporary situation is less directly political (though equally social). This genus that I have yet to nominate has two species that can be referred to as "Ghetto Catholic" and "Cosmopolitan Catholic." These two nonpolitical (or, we should say, *pre*-political) responses are primarily distinguished by the degree of optimism which can be achieved given the particular circumstances. Thus, the Cosmopolitan Catholic perceives his home to be secure and can therefore be engaged in evangelization simply; that is, evangelization of nonbelievers; the Ghetto Catholic recognizes barbarians both outside *and within* his walls and thus at best can only concentrate on a little re-evangelization. For example, I recently heard a homily in which the priest explained that St. Paul did not really understand God's love, for, if he did, he would not have said that God judges. After all, God is love, and love is unconditional forgiveness; God/love never judges. Fortunately, it was a weekday Mass and Father did not have to contradict himself immediately by repeating the words of the creed: "He will come again *to judge* the living and the dead." Some of us, as you see, and to put it bluntly, have no time to go *ad gentes*. The enemy has invaded and is now living with us. The Christian soldier, sword outstretched and back against the tabernacle, finds comfort in St. Michael and is quickened by the blood of the holy martyrs. But such a defensive posture is certainly not necessary for all. The rapid growth of religious groups who are quietly going out and winning converts appears (at least through anecdotal evidence) to be amazing. Pilgrims though we may be in this world, we are not meant to walk alone, and Cosmopolitan Catholics are not solitary walkers.

The last response to the contemporary situation, the "Mosaic" option, is anti-political. This position has much in common with its "Ghetto" brother but is even more pessimistic. This modern Moses finds the American Leviathan too strong to fight politically or legislatively, so a war of words ensues. Public and prolonged attacks go to the very heart of the Republic in an attempt to convince all who hear to be "at war with the regime." This position maintains that there is nothing to defend, that the American experiment was stillborn. Longing to live in the Castilian mountains, or the Alps of Liechtenstein, this Moses contents himself with diatribes. His greatest danger is that the political authorities will take him seriously; for their arms seem to be greater than his. Meanwhile, he continues to lash away, undermining even the natural love of one's own that is necessary for any society.

Evaluating our responses: First questions

In order to think about these different responses and about how we can answer the question of the relationship between being a Catholic and living in an increasingly secular society, it seems to me that the first question ought to be: What does it mean to be a Roman Catholic? Or, to put it another way, "What is the nature and mission of the Church which Christ founded on the rock of Peter and to which we have pledged our very souls?"

This audience will forgive me, I imagine, if I put that question directly to the Church and see what she says; we can talk about her revisionists' hallucinations some other day. Let me give two passages by way of a general answer. The first comes to us from Pope John Paul II in his Post-Synodal Apostolic Exhortation *Christifideles laici*, 33:

> The entire mission of the Church, then, is concentrated and manifested in evangelization. Through the winding passages of history the Church has made her way under the grace of and command of Jesus Christ: 'Go into all the world and preach the gospel to the whole creation' (Mark 16:15)
>
> "To evangelize," writes Paul VI, "is the grace and vocation proper to the Church, her most profound identity" (*Evangelium nuntiandi*, 14).

A little later in that same Exhortation, the Holy Father notes that, in virtue of their baptism and confirmation, each man and woman "is made a sharer in the threefold mission of Jesus Christ Priest, Prophet and King and is thereby charged and given the ability to fulfill the fundamental apostolate of the Church: *evangelization*" (EN, 51).[1]

So there we have it: the Church is to evangelize, and the laity — men and women, whether young or old — are supposed to engage in this mission, this evangelization. Now, the ever-present question: "How?" We begin with a general answer.

General answers

There is a disturbing tendency these days when speaking to others about the Faith to sidestep the Church's teaching when trying to convert (or reconvert) our brothers and sisters, separated or not. Recently, a friend here in Philadelphia picked me up at the airport and was showing me the city and its beautiful architecture. Along the tour, we ended up at a local Catholic college and were greeted by a charming nun who showed us around a particularly striking building. She had been the superior of her congregation and had spent eleven years in western Africa as a missionary. When she asked what I do, I explained that I run an evangelization project. To that news, she could think of only one thing to say: "So, are you an advocate of women's ordination?" "Evangelization" means, at least in her missionary mind, dissent from the Church.

What seems to me to be most important when talking about evangelization, is always to remember the relationship that the Holy Father weaves into his writing; namely, the relationship between evangelization and the Church. In *Christifideles laici*, the Holy Father meditates on the meaning of the parable of the vineyard. All of us are called at various hours to work in the vineyard (CL, 2); but we are called to be more than laborers, we are to become part of the vineyard (CL, 8). Beginning with reference to the Second Vatican Council's *Lumen Gentium*, 6, the pope explains:

> "Christ is the true vine who gives life and fruitfulness to the branches, that is, to us. Through the Church we abide in Christ, without whom we can do nothing (John 15:1-5)." The Church herself, then, is the vine in the gospel. She is *mystery* because the very life and love of the Father, Son and Holy Spirit are the gift gratuitously offered to all those who are born of water and the Holy Spirit (cf. John 3:5), and called to relive the very *communion* of God and to manifest it and communicate it in history (mission): "In that day," Jesus says, "you will know that I am in my Father and you in me, and I in you" (John 14:20).
>
> Only *from inside the Church's mystery of communion is the "identity" of the lay faithful made known*, and their fundamental dignity revealed. Only within the context of this dignity can their vocation and mission in the Church and in the world be defined (CL, 8).

The connection between us, the branches, and the Church, the vine, could not be made more strongly. Without the Church, we are fruitless and perish. What about our life as sharers in the Church's mission to evangelize? What is our specific relation to the Church in that situation? Of the many possible answers, I will mention just two.

First, faith or personal holiness. From Paul VI, we learn that:

The first means of evangelization is the witness of an authentically Christian life, given to God in a communion that nothing should destroy and at the same time given to one's neighbor with limitless zeal. . . . St. Peter expressed this well when he held up the example of a reverent and chaste life that wins over even without a word those who refuse to obey the word. It is therefore primarily by her conduct and by her life that the Church will evangelize the world, in other words, by her living witness of fidelity to the Lord Jesus — the witness of poverty and detachment, of freedom in the face of the powers of this world, in short, the witness of sanctity (EN, 41).[2]

John Paul agrees. In *Redemptoris missio*, 90, he writes:

The call to mission derives, of its nature, from the call to holiness. A missionary is really such only if he commits himself to the way of holiness. "Holiness must be called a fundamental presupposition and an irreplaceable condition for everyone in fulfilling the mission of salvation in the Church" (CL, 17).

That initial conversion, the turning to Christ that normally comes about through this witness, is only the first step. There remains a maturity that can only be found through instruction. In *Catechesi tradendae*, we read that:

The specific character of catechesis, as distinct from the initial conversion-bringing proclamation of the Gospel, has the twofold objective of maturing the initial faith and educating the true disciple of Christ by means of a deeper and more systematic knowledge of the person and the message of our Lord Jesus Christ (CT, 19).

Together, a personal witness of faith and catechesis can be said to make up the core of the life of the evangelist.[3] Evangelists are "followers of Christ and who love the Catholic faith . . . who wish to deepen their own love for Christ and their understanding of Catholic teaching, and to help others to do so as well."[4] Since all of us are called to be evangelists insofar as we are all sons and daughters of the Church, this description should fit all of us.

Catholics' responses: An answer

Let us turn back now to the three responses to the contemporary situation mentioned above: 1) to tell a Noble Lie, 2) to be a Ghetto or Cosmopolitan Catholic, or 3) to flee, like Moses out of Egypt. From a political philosopher's perspective, each of these responses is problematic. Though its adherents take politics seriously, the Noble Lie distorts the true character of this political order in an effort to fend off enemies and rally defenders. The Lie is forced to present only the nobler aspects of the American founding and to turn a blind eye to the correlation between what was given to us in the founding documents and what we have today, as if something nefarious just dropped in from "The X-Files" and perverted our once-proud structure.

At the other extreme, our Moses has abandoned all hope in politics. He takes politics seriously and will readily confess that human beings are political by nature, but the hatred for the evil he sees has also blinded him. He cannot find it in himself to recognize the many benefits that even a corrupted city can bring and is ready to tear down the walls; all consequences be damned.

In the middle, our unnamed herd of Ghetto and Cosmopolitan Catholics are called pre-political because they have little use for politics. They concern themselves with "culture" and "society," and like Aristotle's pre-political man, the one-eyed Cyclops, they fail to see the depths of either. Laws and public education have a profound effect on "culture" and "society," but their limited vision is unable to focus on the deep connection between laws and culture. They are doomed to fight only half of their own battle, seemingly ignorant that more is to be done.

Such are the beginnings of a profane criticism, but what about a response from a more sacred perspective? This question is important because of the Holy Father's consistent emphasis on the "New Evangelization." "New" in this case meaning primarily "renewed" and "taking into consideration the contemporary circumstances." These three responses are reflective of those circumstances and are eminently helpful as we try to take the proper bearing: They help lay out the parameters of the antidote that need to be administered and reveal that solutions with excessive or insufficient regard to politics are doomed. If the foundations of politics lie in the mists of the confluence of nature and super-nature, the rebirth and healing of the political order must as well. Enter the "New Evangelization."

The first response, in so far as it exhibits a tendency to try to "spin" the teachings of the Church in a way that will make them seem more compatible with a political or economic reality than they really are must be avoided. To dumb-down the exultant richness of the Church or to sugarcoat her ancient criticisms of our modern attachments for the sake of a seeming harmony is a disservice to the Truth. We cannot cringe or hide the Truth Who sets us free merely in order to appease some misguided ideological convictions.

Our Mosaic man is ringing with the words of Truth, but they have become the words of anger and hatred, not of love. His guerrilla war sees everyone as his enemy to be battled and no one as his neighbor to be loved. It is a lonely and often sad life, counting victories and losses but not converts. Go out to all the world and preach the Good News? Not for him; it is retreat and dig in.

All of which leaves us with a politically bankrupt reality, whether in the ghetto or the cosmopolis. To the extent that they can, this middle group is trying to fulfill its duties to evangelize. They are good at making the connection between the divine law and one's personal moral code. Moving from the eternal and divine laws to the natural law they have no problem. Going from the eternal, divine, and natural laws to the civil law . . . there's the rub. Souls are saved one at a time, but nature at its best points to the supernatural. If our laws, derived principally from the natural law, do not point in some general way to the supernatural — to the One, True God — then our very nature is undermined. For our nature to be perfected by grace, it only makes sense that we should be attendant to the natural and unnatural things with which we surround ourselves. As we would not stop caring for our bodies because we wanted to focus on our souls, we would be remiss if we were not to carry the teachings of Christ into our natural political associations.

A practical example:
Millennium Evangelization Project

As for the practical means of implementing these teachings specifically in the political realm, I shall defer to the advice of our practiced Catholic statesmen. What I can offer is a complement to their work: a practical example of how the New Evangelization can be carried out by many of us personally in a way that is fully grounded in the teachings of Christ's Church.

In November 1994, the Holy Father wrote *Tertio Millennio Adveniente*, an Apostolic Letter on the coming third millennium. In that letter, he invites the Church universal to prepare actively for the Great Jubilee of the Year 2000. Specifically, he wants us to spend the last three years of this millennium preparing for the Jubilee by following a Trinitarian outline.

At the University of Dallas, the Millennium Evangelization Project has responded to this invitation by developing conferences following the triplex structure. In 1997, our theme will be "Christ Reveals Man to Himself." In 1998, it will be "The Holy Spirit Completing the Mission of God through the Church." In 1999, it will be "God, Father and Creator."

Each year, the Millennium Project is offering to the Church three conferences. For example, in 1997, the three conferences are "Jesus Christ: Revelation of God's Love;" "The Culture of Life vs. The Culture of Death," and "Life in Christ." Our goal, through these conferences, is to make Christ and the richness of His message more widely known and better understood. It is well known that too few Catholics know their Faith well. Consequently, the Millennium Project helps educate Catholics about their Faith so that they can dedicate themselves more fully to him and can, in the face of the modern challenges, evangelize others to follow Christ.

The conference material has two parts. First are the scripts to be presented. Teachers — theological and philosophical exerts —

are writing the scripts that are the basis of the conferences. To guarantee our faithfulness in our presentation of the Church's teaching, all our scripts are sent to a board of Episcopal Advisors for review; the last thing we want or need is to distort in any way the true teaching of Christ's Church. In order to help guarantee our accurate presentation, we are basing the scripts on the *Catechism*, the documents of Vatican II, and on papal encyclicals.

Second, the written word that is given human voice is coupled with engaging visuals. In our highly visual modern world, we have found the addition of multimedia images to be a great benefit in explaining the tenets of our Faith.

That is the material: the catechetical part of our evangelization. As for the personal witness, we are soliciting people all over the country to volunteer to take this material and go out, through their own dioceses, to make these presentations. These lovers of Christ are being trained to take the scripts and, without changing them — after all, we are not in the business of changing the Church's teaching — they are trained to take the scripts and, if you will, make them their own. There is, of course, a huge difference between simply reading something and presenting it. To be a convincing witness and not some dull teacher or lecturer, the scripts have to be given a personality. It takes a little training, but it is surprisingly easy; easy, at least, if one starts with true believers.

Once these speakers have been trained, we send them out, in teams of four, to parishes, schools, and lay groups throughout their diocese. In this way, and under their bishops' guidance, they can serve their local Church. In this way, Christ continues His threefold mission of Priest, Prophet, and King through these threefold activities of His faithful.[5]

There are many ways to respond to the Holy Father's request to engage in a New Evangelization and to prepare for the Millennium. That we are all called, each and every one of us, and that through baptism and confirmation we are each given the ability to respond, these cannot be denied. So let me end with a prayer for you, and for us, as we discern how we will answer this invitation:

Our Lady of Guadalupe, Mother of the Americas, behold how great the harvest is. Intercede before the Lord for us so that our hunger for sanctity in the world may increase.

Queen of the Apostles, accept our complete readiness to work for the restoration and fulfillment of your Son's kingdom. May we not withhold anything at all in helping to bring His salvific Will to fruition. May we be completely dedicated to the cause of the Gospel and be a stimulus for reciprocal charity among men and women and all nations. Amen.

Endnotes

1 Cf. *Lumen Gentium*, Chapter IV.

2. Reference to St. Peter is found in 1 Peter 3:1.

3. Cf. CT, 20.

4. Millennium Evangelization Project Brochure.

5. Cf. *Lumen Gentium*, Chapter IV, esp. para 34-6.

Chapter IX
Reverend Robert A. Sirico, C.S.P.

Subsidiarity:
A Call to Community

The *Catechism of the Catholic Church* states: "The principle of subsidiarity is opposed to all forms of collectivism. It sets limits for state intervention" (1885). The principle of subsidiarity derives primarily from the natural law tradition and Roman Catholic social teaching. But its application is much broader. To some extent, it has found its political expression in the American concept of federalism, and, in Europe, the concept has become a critical part of the debate on the relations between nations and the central authority of the European Community. In these political contexts, the principle has been invoked by the partisans of limited government over centralized management of peoples, states, and nations. As a philosophical notion, it provides an intellectual framework for the rightly-constructed social order rooted in the Christian faith and human liberty.

Today, the principle of subsidiarity is a crucial, if largely tacit, part of our common understanding of the components of a free and virtuous society: power and authority resides among the many various units that are most capable of carrying out its functions properly within the context of human rights and human freedom.

The thesis of the subsidiarity principle is at once simple, deeply meaningful, and socially significant. Quoting from *Centesimus Annus*, the *Catechism of the Catholic Church* says, "A community of a higher order should not interfere in the internal life of a community of a lower order, depriving the latter of its functions, but rather should support it in case of need and help to coordinate its activity with the activities of the rest of society, always with the view to the common good" (1883). The concept posits a hierarchy of social action and responsibility that begins

81

with the claim of primacy for the smallest units in society, including individuals, families, and community associations. These groups have the first responsibility for caring for their needs and those with whom they come in contact. On the occasion when they fail to function as they should, higher social structures, beginning with the closest level of government, are permitted to assume responsibility for those same functions, but only for the duration that the higher orders can perform the job more effectively than can the lower ones. If higher-order intervention takes places in absence of systemic failure, lower orders are forcibly divested of what they do best, the common good of all suffers, and the principle of subsidiarity has been violated.

The meaning of subsidiarity is derived from the Latin *subsidium,* meaning to help or to aid. This root implies that fundamental to the principle is that a permanent state of usurpation of one function by another order (e.g. the government, and not the family, rearing children) is to be ruled out. Higher orders can intervene in the affairs of the lower ones only as auxiliary aids and never permanent substitutes, and only then under certain circumstances. Moreover the authority between spheres of influence and power within society are internally legitimate and not merely derivative. The state, for example, is more suited to the provision of national defense and the authority for its provision is not necessarily derived from other institutions.

Similarly, the family exercises authority which is suitable to its structure and place in society, and that authority is neither delegated to nor approved by higher authorities. Johannes Messner says that the principle of subsidiarity does not imply society is bound to provide certain social services in all possible contingencies, but rather illuminates the division of competencies among social institutions.[1]

Societies which adhere to the principle of subsidiarity create and maintain a bottom-up social structure, with the departure point being families and community relations. Higher orders are the resources of last resort only. "The principle of subsidiarity," says the *Catechism*, "is opposed to all forms of collectivism. It sets limits for state intervention." The purpose of the principle is not to isolate spheres of influence within society, but through the exercise of human freedom and justice to harmonize "the relations between individuals and societies." Paradoxically, this harmony "tends toward the establishment of true international order" (1885).

A society respecting the principle of subsidiarity contrasts with a top-down model of society in which the central government presumes to have the primary role in ordering people's lives.

The latter only delegates power when lower orders will carry out functions in accordance with the government's overall plan. "Just as it is wrong to withdraw from the individual and commit to a group what private enterprise and industry can accomplish," writes Pius XI in 1931 in *Quandragesimo Anno*, this century's most famous statement of the subsidiarity principle, "so too it is an injustice, a grave evil and a disturbance of right order for a larger and higher association to arrogate to itself functions which can be performed efficiently by smaller and lower societies. This is a fundamental principle of social philosophy, unshaken, and unchangeable" (#79-80).

Experience teaches us that the top-down model operates at the expense of practicality, creativity, and liberty. "Excessive intervention by the state," says the *Catechism*, "can threaten personal freedom and initiative" (1883). The purpose of the subsidiarity principle, in contrast, is to establish a way of thinking about social life that has a high regard for the freedom of individuals, families, and communities; for creativity in responding to particular needs and situations; and for the best performance of social tasks like caring for society's weakest members.

An additional argument for the subsidiarity principle comes from another intellectual tradition that developed in the second half of this century. It began with the writings of F.A. Hayek, and in particular, his insight regarding the use of knowledge in society. In Hayek's understanding, the information necessary for the well-functioning of society is necessarily dispersed among individuals and the various organic units of society. It is not practicable for all the knowledge necessary for society to work to be accumulated in central units of society, much less in the minds of single individuals presuming to plan society.[2] This argument was first deployed against socialism, but in its development it grew to impact our conception of how social democratic and even market-oriented societies function. Hayek's insight regarding the necessary dispersion of knowledge helps guard against the temptation of the higher and political orders to over take and eventually swamp lower and private orders within nations, and points to the loss society incurs if they do.

The subsidiarity principle also informs religious concerns. If we can agree that values and morals make up the indispensable bulwark of sustaining a viable social order, and that the religious traditions of the West are the essential framework in which to understand and fully express those values and morals, we need some transmission mechanism to impart religious values to those in society that do not accept them due to unfortunate circumstances (alienation, rejection, dependency, etc.) That mechanism is evangelization: bringing the good news of Christ to people and cultures unfamiliar with the Faith and inspiring them towards belief and the practice of faith in their lives. The subsidiarity principle helps in this regard because the people most capable of evangelizing nonbelievers are the Christians closest to them.

The loss of the evangelical function of the lower orders has been one of the most costly aspects of the modern tendency toward centralization. If the principle of subsidiarity is ignored by society, the teaching authority of the family and the Church is not exercised as well as it could be. That means that values and morals essential to the thriving of civilization are not transmitted to new generations.

The loss of values and morals, occasioned by the transfer of rightful authority to higher and less capable orders, is the primary cultural, political, and moral characteristic of our times. The means to regain those values and morals is a greater cultural appreciation of the virtue of subsidiarity and a greater institutional recognition of the central place it must have in right ordering of the economic and political culture.

"The family," says the *Catechism*, "is the original cell of social life" (2207) and the essential bulwark of a free and well-ordered society. The family serves as the crucial means of acculturation and the key to transmitting values from generation to generation, and it is the family that enables us to make good use of freedom. Yet contemporary public policy has served both to interfere with and assume the functions of the family, with an obvious example being government-assistance solutions for children born out of wedlock. The consequence of government solutions has been a dramatic increase in the incidence of illegitimacy, as fathers, in particular, are no longer needed to support their biological families.

The subsidiarity principle informs our view of the government's relation to family policy, making the centralization the last thirty years indefensible. Far from having corrected grave problems in society's lower orders, the higher orders have intervened and usurped the prerogatives of the family and community to the detriment of all. In the case of economic need and other forms of social deprivation, if these problems had been addressed at the local level, the need of families would have been met apart from the materialistic assumption at the root of the modern welfare state.

With regard to evangelization, there are few better opportunities for imparting values and faith than family intervention by churches and community groups. Through personal contact with the poor, weak, and disadvantaged, the Church can present a more authentic and credible witness for Christ in their lives. Part of what has been perceived as a decline in the vibrancy of the witness of the Church in recent years is due to a loss of a sense of mission. This is due to losing (or surrendering) to the federal government the crucial function of caring for families in need.

As it stands under current policy, in many cases the Church has been crowded out by the federal government in a number of areas. Consider abortion. With *Roe* v. *Wade,* the Supreme Court invalidated the laws of every state and locality in the country and imposed a uniform code which effectively legalized the systematic and arbitrary destruction of the life of the unborn. In doing so, the Court not only violated the principle of subsidiarity, it codified into our nation's law the idea that courts and government, not community and Church, are to be the arbiters of the structure of family ethics. The result has been to enshrine principles of sexual license and family breakup at the expense of traditional morality and marital commitment.

The same is true of welfare for the less fortunate. In a recent invocation of the principle of subsidiarity, Pope John Paul II writes of the failure of the modern state. "Malfunctions and defects in the Social Assistance State," he writes in *Centesimus Annus*, "are the result of an inadequate understanding of the task proper to the State" (#48). The pope points to a practical cost of violating subsidiarity: the politicization of society. Public agencies proliferate at the expense of smaller communities of charity and enterprise.

The costs of the welfare state have indeed not only been economic to the extent that bureaucracy always grows at the expense of a dynamic exchange economy. The cost is also moral, because of the welfare state pursues its takes in terms of a moral code increasingly alien from traditional Christian tenants. For example, the very concept of a welfare "entitlement" runs contrary to the scriptural understanding of aiding the poor: Helping others is a moral duty that springs from spiritual commitment and is not essentially exercised through coercion or government mandates. The modern, central state has proven itself incapable of distinguishing between the deserving and the undeserving poor, and between aid that fosters independence and moral development from that which reinforces a dependency mind-set and moral nihilism. The distinction between the two can only be revealed to those in need through the evangelization function of the Church and community.

Consider the case of an out-of-wedlock birth. Members of the parish become aware of the complexity of the problems. They come to understand the personal circumstances, strengths and weaknesses, and resources available to the household. Where the government offers checks, one-size-fits-all programs, and distant bureaucrats, the Church offers love, personal encouragement, creative solutions, and, when necessary, specifically catered services and material aid. Church members can be involved in solutions that strengthen marital, family, and neighborhood bonds instead of weakening them. Their goal is to help individuals live moral lives as independent members of the Church and community.

Subsidiarity must be applied to education as well. Once the

education of children was entirely a function of the local community and the states, but is now, to an alarming extent, a social task undertaken by the federal government. It is not only the constant and looming presence of the federal Department of Education which is objectionable. It is the very idea that federal dollars would have such a major impact over something as intimate and family-related as the education of children. Whether we move towards a voucher system or a radical decentralization of education, the primary goal of a social policy based on the subsidiarity principle must be to give parents and local communities a greater degree of control over their children's education. And given the unparalleled success of the Catholic Church in providing education in the United States, Catholic schools must necessarily play a large role — whether institutionally or as providing tested models — in the future of an education system based on the idea of subsidiarity.

As a final application of the subsidiarity principle, we should mention the general notion that the free enterprise economy is an institution that both requires and reinforces traditional moral concerns. Entrepreneurship is linked to the virtue of creativity. Trade, exchange, and contract are bound up with the idea of promise keeping. Private property, the foundation of the free market, represents the institutional embodiment of the commandment to respect the private ownership of what belongs to oneself and to one's neighbor. Even when the relations among traders and property owners results in large institutions like multinational corporations, the subsidiarity principle is recognized and fulfilled in institutions like individual stockholders and consumers who are the main determinants of market signals like profit and loss. Indeed, it is through large and complex economic, cultural, and social networks, based on market exchange, that the essential aim of subsidiarity can be achieved: "the establishment of true international order" (*Catechism*, 1885).

Today, those called to practice charity and to exercise concerns for others find themselves living in a society that has insufficient respect for the principle of subsidiarity. While it is true that the central government has crowded out the lower orders and has restricted opportunities for charity, that in no way relieves us of our moral obligations. The *Catechism* is without qualifications when it insists that "there are many families who are at times incapable" of caring for the young, the old, the sick, the disabled, and the poor. "It devolves then on other persons, other families, and, in a subsidiary way, society to provide for their needs" (*Catechism*, 2208).

There are many practical ways that Americans today, even though we live under a government that provides little opportunity, can creatively exercise the virtue of charity. This is especially true in our communities of faith, as the existence of hundreds of thousands of local and church-based charities demonstrates. One ministry that has worked to help welfare mothers become independent has been a buddy system, linking people in suburban and urban churches. Support teams from the suburbs comprised of three to six church members offer friendship, spiritual and moral encouragement, practical advice, baby-sitting and material help to mothers who are on welfare. Through their friendship, many women have been able to overcome drug dependency, find employment, and extricate themselves from abusive relationships.[3]

There are other opportunities for helping single-parent families. In many urban areas, latchkey children have no one supervising their after school hours, so homework often goes unfinished. Parishes can set up study halls in the afternoon hours that are supervised by a teacher paid by the parish board. Parish members can volunteer to assist. There can be a nominal fee for recipient families. This would keep kids off the streets and in an environment conducive to study.[4]

Parish members can also involve themselves in abortion counseling for women with out-of-wedlock pregnancies. Many already do, but this ministry needs to be expanded. Volunteers in crisis pregnancy centers present women with the true facts about abortion and alternatives to it. They help mothers plan their lives after the birth. If mothers desire to give the children up, they introduce them to adoption agencies. Such organizations can also provide material aid before and after birth.

These are just a few possibilities parishes can try in their own communities. Once the idea of the subsidiarity principle is understood, one cannot help but be impressed by how many contemporary social and spiritual difficulties could be addressed and even solved by paying it greater attention in our private lives and in public affairs. Not only does subsidiarity provide for a more workable social model than the central state in such areas as family life, welfare, education, and enterprise. It provides a perfect opportunity for the sharing of the Gospel with people in our parishes and communities. A society that recognizes subsidiarity is also a society that provides its members the greatest possible opportunity for sharing the Good News of the Faith with others.

Endnotes

1. *Social Ethics* (St. Louis: B. Herder Book Co., 1958).
2. "The Uses of Knowledge in Society" in *Individualism and the Economic Order* (Chicago: Gateway, 1972), pp. 77-91.
3. Amy L. Sherman, "The Buddy System: Personal Friendship is a Poverty-fighting Tool," *World* (January 6, 1996, p. 21).
4. Ceasar A. Arredonde, "Help the Poor Now: A Practical Plan," *Crisis*, February 1995, p. 14.

Chapter X
Mercedes Wilson

Upholding the Dignity of Women: Witnessing to the Truth in Istanbul

I have been asked to present to you the hidden drama that has been taking place at the recent United Nations conferences. It would seem logical and proper to believe that the unanimous goal in all these conferences should be to attain a common operative effort to defend the dignity of men and women and the promotion of their universal human rights. Unfortunately, this is not the case.

In all of these U.N. conferences, the western delegates have a shown a pronounced difficulty in using the word "family" in almost any context in the documents. The Cairo conference demonstrated this difficulty ironically, during the U.N. declared "Year of the Family." In Beijing, the anti-family coalition aggressively sought to remove from the U.N. Platforms for Action all reference to religion, spirituality, morals, or ethics — except when they were portrayed negatively, such as when associated with intolerance or extremism. There is a strange kind of "familiophobia" at work in the mind-set of those preparing such U.N. documents.

The ideological dogma created by radical population controllers was neither written nor influenced by the right people. Rather than turning to the moral/religious and civic leaders of our time, undue influence seems to have been given to organizations like the International Planned Parenthood Federation. Such groups have convinced First World governments that population control is critical and that the end justifies the means, even if barbaric practices are instituted to achieve it. It is clear that the Platforms for Action would be radically different if the true leaders (not just political) of the world had been involved in its writing.

"All that is needed for evil to prevail is for good people to do nothing," wrote Edmund Burke. This is precisely what is happening today. The political leaders and legislators of the western world seem to be technologically brilliant, but spiritually shallow and morally bankrupt. So they bow down to pressure from powerful special-interest groups to legislate against the family.

It has been tragic to observe the progressive changes during these meetings. At first, various delegates from the developing countries openly and enthusiastically supported the inclusion of desperately needed language that defended the rights of parents over their children, upheld the vocation of motherhood, supported *self-control* instead of *birth-control* for adolescents and preadolescents, opposed female feticide, demanded a clear definition of the term "gender" as *"the two sexes of the human being,"* and much more.

However, as delegates from the powerful First World nations perceived a mini-revolt emerging — when a few courageous delegates from the little republics dared to voice their opinion and tried to clearly define such words as "gender," the western countries' delegates became alarmed. Such deviations from their anti-life, anti-family agenda demanded a quick change in the rules of the game! Suddenly we heard that meetings were postponed, voting was halted, the date of the meeting's conclusion was extended, and a full month was booked exclusively to study the definition of "gender," which should have taken only five minutes to resolve. The western countries' delegates engaged in powerful lobbying on the poor nations' delegates who dared to speak out in defense of the family and its future. For instance, my own Guatemalan ambassador received phone calls from the office of the secretary general of the United States, complaining about his outspoken delegate who dared to request that the term "gender" be clearly defined. Our foreign minister received a threatening letter last year from the U.S. ambassador implying that my continuing outspokenness may threaten U.S. assistance to Guatemala. Some delegates were directly approached by the U.S. delegation, while many others received pressure from the European delegations. This was not democracy at work. It was coercion and manipulation in practice.

The consequences that followed were indeed tragic. One by one, my friends and supporters backed down as the voting began, even those who supported us and coauthored the clear definition of "gender" as "the existence of woman and man as the two sexes of the human being." When we asked one of these delegates why he had changed his position, he apologized and said: "I am sorry, but the U.S. delegation is putting so much pressure on my country that I am no longer able to support you." Some told us that their ambassadors had given them instructions to remain silent and not to support me. Others would confidentially agree with our position, but were afraid of reprisals on their international loans that would affect their country's economy if they openly voiced their opinion. As a result, a non-definition passed. "Gender," it was decided, means whatever you want it to mean — one, two, or three sexes.

Habitat II

As a veteran of four United Nations conferences, I knew exactly what to expect from the western countries' delegates at the Habitat II conference in Istanbul. I knew what the reaction would be when we requested that innocent words like "mother," "parents," "family," or even the inclusion of the word "man" be added to the conference documents. Immediately, the United States, the European Union, Canada, and Norway jumped in to request that the above stated words be deleted. However, the little mouse that roared, usually Guatemala, the Holy See, the Moslem countries, Argentina, and a few African countries, insisted on keeping such fundamental language in the document as necessary definitions for the inhabitants of what the U.N. calls "human settlements." Because such words are subject to dispute by those with a feminist or homosexual agenda, they are immediately bracketed for the purpose of being negotiated in more confidential, closed-door meetings. This allows the western delegations time to exert pressure on the poor nations who disagree with those agendas, with the added advantage that no outsiders, including the press, be present.

But this time it was different. A curious phenomenon occurred in Istanbul — the developing countries were united as never before. Every time the western countries tried to impose language contrary to our culture and traditions, they were quickly silenced. It was delightful to see them on the run as we determined our next move with India, Indonesia, the Arab nations, and Argentina. The delegations I just mentioned were not the usual bureaucrats who are more worried about their jobs or their country not receiving that long-awaited loan from the World Bank or the International Monetary Fund, or the danger of not getting the humanitarian aid so desperately needed in many poor countries of the world. This time the delegates, and rightly so, were in the main composed more of ministers, vice-ministers, or staff involved in housing and planning. Not being knowledgeable of the decadent workings of these United Nations conferences, the developing countries' delegates thought that this conference would be dealing with the complexities of human settlements, rather than introducing reproductive rights, sexual rights, population control, or replacing parental rights with children's rights.

The draft document for Habitat II was produced by the "western" countries (American and Canadian influence is obvious and strong). The impact of these two nations on the conference is evidenced by the influence of Bella Abzug, who was highly praised by the president of the conference, Mr. Wally N'Dow of Kenya, as he presided over the closing of the conference. He openly betrayed any trace of mystery as to who is really commanding these conferences by toeing the line to the western nations. These U.N. documents are a full-scale attack on the whole philosophical-theological-cultural tradition of the West which the western powers seem intent to dramatically change. It is an ideological combination of materialist and state-of-nature anthropology, combined with new age psychology, radical egalitarianism, and gender feminism.

The contraceptive mentality

The biggest conflict at the recent U.N. conferences revolved around the term "reproductive health." This battle, pitting the world's most powerful western countries against its most weak and

93

impoverished, entailed changing cultural values and religious traditions worldwide. Following are some of the arguments I presented to the western delegates, but to no avail.

It is high time to recognize that, historically, every country that has embraced the contraceptive mentality has inevitably succumbed to the legalization of abortion. Furthermore, national and international population control programs — which ignore cultural and religious traditions of peoples throughout the world — are not only very expensive for the taxpayers, but very lucrative for the industries involved. To the poor countries of the developing world it becomes a financial nightmare. While the West can absorb the enormous medical costs associated with artificial birth control, lesser developed countries, who can barely treat common diseases, are unable to cope with the expenses of treating the many serious side effects that result from the use of artificial birth control. The international programs have been dismal failures — heartbreaking and destructive to the people of the Third World. As the influence of such programs spreads, so do divorce rates and other socially troubling behavior.

Dr. Nafis Sadik, Executive Director of the United Nations Population Fund, mentions the issue of "reproductive health" in the following excerpt from her speech delivered on August 9, 1996, to the Canada-U.S.A. Women's Health Forum entitled "Women's Health: Beyond Cairo and Beijing":

> For the developing countries, the ICPD [Cairo] Programme of Action estimates that providing reproductive health care, as well as collecting and analyzing population data, will cost $17.0 billion by the year 2000, and $21.7 billion in 2015. Two thirds of the cost will be borne by the developing countries themselves; one third must come from external sources. The $5.7 billion required in 2000 is more than three times what the donor community provided in 1994.

I can assure you that the poor countries are not only unaware that they will incur the cost of two-thirds of programs that will continue destroying their people physically, morally, and spiritually, but how can they afford to continue going bankrupt?

The time has come for the truth to unfold with regard to the so-called "humanitarian" family planning programs that are nothing more than chemical warfare against women and families. The people of the Third World have always been pressured to accept such pernicious programs. I can assure you there is nothing humane about them.

Time and again I demanded that women should be properly informed of such abuses, reminding the delegates that the Beijing Conference was supposed to be for the benefit of women. Nevertheless, my petitions were repeatedly denied, my factual information from U.S. government sources was ignored, and my requests that programs of abstinence and the promotion of self control instead of birth control be implemented, was continuously ridiculed.

Artificial methods of birth control

Artificial birth control has turned into a billion-dollar industry that benefits pharmaceutical companies, doctors, and population control organizations. In fact, the contraceptive mentality has so permeated western cultures that doctors generally fail to inform their patients of all the dangers to their health and the abortifacient effect of the many methods of artificial birth control.

These include the most commonly used methods, such as the Pill, Norplant (six tiny silicone capsules inserted under the skin just above the elbow providing five years of research), Depo-Provera (a three-month contraceptive injection), and the intrauterine device (IUD), all of which were first experimented on the poor in Third World countries. The artificial birth control industry ignores studies which show a link between the hormones in such contraceptive chemicals and a significant increase in cancer among women, as well as numerous other serious consequences. Frequently, women in the Third World are not told of the side effects of the various contraceptive methods. These adverse reactions are usually more severe for poor women than for women in the West due to malnourishment and generally poor health.

In addition, bioethicists, sociologists, educators, and concerned citizens have expressed concern that Norplant could be used as a tool of government social policy. Lawmakers in more than a dozen states have proposed legislation aimed at using Norplant to control reproduction among welfare recipients, criminal offenders, and so forth — all in the name of reducing public costs. There is significant potential for abuse of government power in this area. The same could be said for Depo-Provera.

Furthermore, serious medical and ethical questions have been raised about the Norplant system. The manufacturer, Wyeth-Ayerst, disputes the connection between Norplant and the symptoms reported, but tens of thousands of women around the United States are involved in lawsuits alleging that side effects were down-played and removal was much more complicated than they were led to believe. In fact, according to the Population Information Program of the Johns Hopkins University, while the Norplant and Norplant 2 systems are designed to be effective for five to seven years respectively, approximately thirty percent of women had had the rods removed by the end of one year, and seventy percent had done so by year five.

A video documentary filmed by the British Broadcasting Corporation discusses the testing of various forms of birth control on Third World women. The video is entitled "The Human Laboratory."

[T]hrough [BBC's] moving filmed testimony, HORIZON uncovers a catalogue of claims that Norplant is destroying women's lives. Serious side effects have been reported. . . . The film follows the diminutive Farida Akhter [executive director of a women's health group] on her mission of mercy through the slums of Dhaka to uncover what she believes is the truth of the [Norplant] trials: side effects not often reported; women pleading for removal of Norplant, but being turned away or asked to pay large sums of money; claims that they did not even know it was an experimental drug. . . . Farida Akhter says: "It's cheaper for them to use Third World women than to use an animal in a laboratory in the West."

It is a tragedy to admit that despite notable technological progress in the past twenty years, scientists have chosen to ignore the basic laws of nature. Huge sums of money have been used by governments and pharmaceutical companies to develop technology that either disrupts normal bodily functions and/or mutilates or destroys reproductive capabilities in favor of sexual pleasure and irresponsible behavior, not the enhancement of true love in marriage.

HIV/AIDS and the fallacy of 'safe sex'

Not only have terms used in the Platforms for Action of these U.N. documents been craftily and strategically selected, important language designed to benefit and protect families and the poor were omitted. For example, health problems related to sexual life (reproductive health, sexually transmitted diseases, fertility control, etc.) are mentioned in the Beijing document more than four hundred times. Yet tropical diseases are mentioned only twice.

While the World Health Organization estimates, for example, four million cases of HIV infection in 1994, the same organization estimates the cases of tropical diseases during the same period as hovering between 650 and 850 million. While HIV is a deadly infection, many others are killing men, women, and their children as well, but they are virtually ignored in the document.

The American Life League's publication entitled: "Condoms and AIDS Fact Sheet: 1995 Update" added the following:

> Some have claimed that the association of HIV with sperm would prevent the virus from passing through the pores of a condom, thereby permitting "safe sex."
>
> This is misleading:
>
> The virus does not always attach to a sperm cell. It can move independently and can easily fit through the pores of a condom.

Like HIV/AIDS, sexually transmitted diseases (STD) are also widespread in today's society. A booklet published by the American College of Obstetricians and Gynecologists in 1991, reported the following frightening facts regarding sexually transmitted diseases:

- STDs are the most common diseases in America next to the common cold and flu.
- 1 in 5 Americans are [sic] presently infected with an STD.
- 12 million new STD cases are reported each year — 33,000/day.
- 45 million Americans are infected with an incurable STD.

According to a "Special Intelligence Report" of January, 1989, in *Parade Magazine*, federal officials and condom makers were shocked by such poor test results that showed that one out of five condom batches failed to meet U.S. standards. The failure rate was unexpectedly high.

Sterilization

Sterilization destroys the beautiful potential for men and women to be procreators of new human beings with immortal souls and destinies. It also has numerous side effects for both men and women.

Too many women have been made objects of systematic sterilization programs which take place in developing countries. Such practices constitute a grave violation of the rights of women which the western delegates were pretending to defend.

While female sterilization is the most popular contraceptive method for women thirty and over, and the second most popular for women 25 to 29, its 0.4 percent failure rate, as reported in the September 1996 issue of *Scientific American*, has now become questionable. This rate represents the number of unintended pregnancies that occurred up to a year after tubal ligation. A 1996 study done by the Centers for Disease Control and Prevention has found that a surprising number of pregnancies occur many years after the surgery. This study of 10,685 women found that the long-term failure rate (the number of pregnancies within ten years) was almost five times the stated rate and that two methods of sterilization — bipolar coagulation and spring clip — had a pregnancy rate of five percent among women who had had the surgery before the age of twenty-eight. One-third of the women who became pregnant suffered ectopic pregnancies — a potentially life-threatening complication.

The evil of abortion

When life is no longer respected or valued from its beginning, why shouldn't it be terminated when pleasure, autonomy, and productivity have ended? Abortion, unthinkable a mere thirty years ago, has become the most commonly performed "surgical procedure" in the United States and the rest of the western world. The medical profession should be up in arms rather than embracing and promoting what they have pledged to oppose: "first do no harm." The most dangerous place for a baby today is the mother's womb. A few decades ago, an abortionist would be put in jail for his crime; today, those who protest abortion nonviolently are the ones being punished and incarcerated.

Pornography and violence

Other damaging influences on human morality and decency that these conferences have been hesitant to attack, are pornography and violence in movies, television, books, magazines, and music distributed worldwide. Any attempt to hold the entertainment industry accountable is immediately dismissed as an attack on freedom of expression or, God forbid, censorship! I think censorship is a wonderful idea. I believe censorship is a necessary component for today's entertainment industry. It does not require expensive studies or research, only common sense, to conclude that these influences are among the leading causes of the deterioration of morals and values within the family and the increase of abuse in the home and violence on the streets.

hCG vaccine

In a field trial prior to marketing it for general use, a fertility regulating vaccine (FRV) is being injected with tetanus toxoid into young women in India, the Philippines, and Latin America. According to a World Health Organization document, the vaccine (antihuman chorionic gonadotrophin (hCG) is being injected without the strict controls imposed on such experiments by most developed countries where governments regulate the introduction of new vaccines to ensure that there are no serious, unwanted side effects. During the closed door negotiations, we fought very hard to include language to stop these abuses against the poor.

The following are excerpts from an article by Paul Borraccia, published in the July/August 1996 issue of *Health Freedom News*.

There has been a vaccine unleashed on an unsuspecting public that has quite another purpose, population control. It is in the guise of a disease preventive vaccine. The hCG vaccine is an abortifacient vaccine — meaning to produce abortion.

Human chorionic gonadotropin is a naturally occurring hormone. It is the messenger that signals a woman's body that she has become pregnant. hCG is also essential for maintaining pregnancy, and its elevated levels can be measured.

The fundamental principal behind the hCG vaccine is to prevent the recognition of pregnancy by the body. The goal, in essence, is to "kill the messenger" by producing antibodies that target and destroy a woman's naturally occurring hCG. In the absence of hCG's message, signaling the presence of an embryo and the process of preparing the uterine environment to embrace the fertilized egg, menstruation occurs and terminates the pregnancy in its earliest stages.

The way in which hCG is "bound into service" against itself, is by injecting hCG, coupled with a tetanus or diphtheria toxoid as a carrier. While generating antibodies against the toxoid, the body is tricked into also generating antibodies against hCG. The body has now been programmed to destroy what would otherwise be recognized as a friend.

The BBC documentary confirms these injurious programs are taking place: "There are several research programmes around the world testing whether a contraceptive can be combined with tetanus or other vaccines and carried into the body to provoke an immune response. The vaccine contains Beta hCG, part of a hormone necessary for pregnancy. By provoking an immune response to both the tetanus and Beta hCG, a woman's own natural hormone is destroyed and pregnancy cannot occur."

Developing countries use a tetanus vaccine laced with hCG as a way to control population growth. In "The Human Laboratory," Dr. Reynaldo Echavez discusses this vaccine being used on women in the Philippines. He says: "We in the Philippine Medical Association don't believe in what the government is saying. The test that were made in both big medical centres were all positive for hCG, Beta hCG, and they claim this is insignificant. To me this could not be insignificant because it can produce anti-hCG. At the moment there is a presence of hCG in the vaccine. It can produce anti-hCG and this can now neutralise the hCG that a woman will produce during pregnancy and abortion will set in."

What is even more frightening is the fact that many western countries have given millions of dollars for the purpose of testing and experimenting with hCG. Dr. Borraccia lists several countries who have given financial support for further development of the drug.

Sweden	$90,000,000
United Kingdom	$52,000,000
Norway	$41,000,000
Denmark	$27,000,000
Germany	$12,000,000
United States	$ 8,200,000

The overpopulation myth

According to an article in *Scientific America's* September 1996 edition, world fertility rates have dropped dramatically. This drop is due in large part, the article states, due to modern methods of birth control.

Those countries that have fertility rates below replacement

level and those approaching that goal are being commended by current administrations and current sociologies. In fact, many developed nations have reached the point of demographic suicide. Many developing countries have no system for caring for the elderly — children are expected to care for their aging parents — so having many children is a form of Social Security. People in these situations reject the notion that it is better to have fewer children. Even when modern contraceptive methods are available, they are often rejected.

Population is not the problem; some of the most densely populated countries in the world are also some of the most prosperous, with the highest levels of economic growth. Conversely, some of the more sparsely populated areas of the developing world experience severe hardships. For example, the population density (in terms of population per square kilometer) in Hong Kong (5,551), Japan (327), Germany (254), and the United Kingdom (234) exceeds that of Haiti (215), Nigeria (117), China (112), and Brazil (18).

I called *Scientific American* to point out the inaccuracies in their unfounded praise of artificial birth control and asked if they would be interested in publishing an article on Natural Family Planning. Their reply was, "Not really. I don't think we would be interested at all!"

We are living in a world where a minority of powerful groups and individuals are imposing a secular humanist doctrine upon the rest of the world. The sagacious ways in which these powerful adversaries disguise their programs as benevolent protectors of the family are repugnant. The majority of the citizens of the West are unaware that this culture of death, funded with their own taxes, is contributing to their own destruction. In addition, the depletion of the western population has been forced below replacement level. According to the U.S. Census Bureau world population profile of 1994, the population of the world begins its decline at the beginning of the next century, at which time it is predicted that the western world's retirement systems will tumble.

The West already does not have enough taxpaying young people to finance the retirement of each retiree. Hence, the next step of the culture of death advocates will be to eliminate the elderly and handicapped by officially legalizing euthanasia through the subtle arguments of "death with dignity" and "living wills." Just as the West legalized the killing of the unborn child, they are rushing to pass the legalization of the elimination of the elderly, disabled, and infirm through euthanasia.

This mentality is devastating the developed world by reducing population to below replacement levels. It also violates and desecrates human dignity and the basic principles of wisdom, morality, reason, and Christianity.

Now that I have presented to you what the culture of death is doing in our own world, we must rise up, denounce it for what it is and bring to the world the culture of life through the following teachings of the wisdom of our Catholic Church and her courageous leader, Pope John Paul the great, who calls Natural Family Planning the "authentic alternative."

Introduction to Natural Family Planning

During the lengthy negotiations at the various U.N. conferences, I specifically mentioned the unfairness of submitting women in particular to the slavery of artificial methods of birth control when women are only fertile for about one hundred hours each cycle. I further insisted that we encourage the natural alternative that respects the autonomy and dignity of the couple — an alternative that is cheaper, safer, scientifically proven, and more culturally acceptable.

I was able to include Natural Family Planning (NFP) in the chapter on health in one of the paragraphs where the U.N. document advocated providing "financial and institutional support for research on safe, effective and affordable technologies for reproductive and sexual health of women and men, including more safe and effective methods." I promptly added, "like Natural Family Planning." This was immediately bracketed by the U.S. delegate with the remark, "I have to check and see if this is an acceptable method of family planning." The Australian and Norwegian delegates whose specialty was to bracket the word "mother" every time I suggested it be added to the document, remarked, "It is not natural to have to abstain anyway." I argued that a few days of abstinence is not an impossibility for a loving couple. Furthermore, we should help governments encourage the use of this new method of Natural Family Planning (NFP) — the ovulation method — for the following reasons:

- It teaches women of all cultural levels to recognize their few days of fertility.
- It is extremely effective and always under the control of a couple.
- A recent study of NFP of 19,843 couples from Calcutta, India, was published in the *British Medical Journal* of September 13, 1993. It confirmed an effectiveness rate of 99.06% for avoiding pregnancy — far superior to any artificial method of birth control. This study was sponsored by the World Health Organization and included Hindu, Moslem, and Christian couples.
- A study of the ovulation method in the People's Republic of China, conducted by the Chinese government, obtained similar results among couples of no religious conviction (98.7% effective). The most impressive result of the study was the continuation rate — 93 percent after the first twelve months. This is the highest continuation rate ever recorded for any method of family planning.
- Artificial methods of birth control such as the Pill and IUD have a fifty percent dropout rate after twelve months among strong and healthy Americans. Women of marginal health in the developing world have a much higher discontinuation rate. Already weak and anemic, they often cannot tolerate the excessive bleeding caused by the abortifacient effect of IUDs, Norplant, or injectable contraceptives. The side effects of the Pill are even more severe. The high discontinuation rates of artificial methods of birth control make it even more costly and wasteful to taxpayers. In contrast, the ovulation method has a ninety-three percent continuation rate.

Research in 1962 by leading Australian and New Zealand

scientists, Dr. John Billings and Dr. James Brown, first validated the ovulation method for the scientific community. Dr. Brown, the originator of hormonal measurements in women, conducted studies of the relationship between women's cervical secretion patterns and ovarian hormonal patterns associated with ovulation.

After thousands of women's cycles in all reproductive categories were tested, Dr. Brown found that the development of the natural signs coordinated with the estrogen levels in the follicular phase of the cycle much better than any other symptom accompanying ovulation.

Success rates are high in the Third World, as well as in the western world: ninety-eight to ninety-nine percent effectiveness for everyone. And the ovulation method is completely natural.

"Science reveals to us that the natural regulation of births is not only possible but fully effective," says the late Professor Jerome Lejeune, discoverer of the genetic basis of Down Syndrome and Director of Research and Fundamental Genetics at the Faculty of Medicine in Paris, France. He continues, "any woman can recognize the signs of her fertility by learning what to look for. This awareness of fertility is the basis for the true freedom of love."

Professor LeJeune also once said: "For NFP to succeed, it requires two basic elements, the husband must love the wife and he must respect her physiology." By respecting the natural functions of the human body, and being able to space children through the natural regulation of conception, a couple increases communication and respect for each other, resulting in dramatically low divorce rates (between two and five percent).

Sex education without morals and values

Sex education programs without morals and values for adolescents, combined with access to artificial birth control clinics, are perhaps the most injurious and perverse of all the plans proposed and being imposed by these U.N. conferences. The concept of adolescent rights was first introduced in Cairo where, fortunately, the objective was not achieved because many countries regarded it as an issue relating to parental authority.

Many delegates of the developing world at U.N. conferences

are realizing what is being done to them. In the Beijing document, forty-seven reservations were placed against issues such as reproductive health — the most reservations in U.N. history at a U.N. conference. Even more remarkable is that these reservations — really objections — were raised primarily by the developing nations. In contrast, only twenty-nine reservations were placed against the Cairo document. Fewer than a quarter of the countries supporting the Cairo document had made any attempt to implement it. At Habitat II in Istanbul, the provisions on reproductive health and sexuality were defeated with one exception, which later was carefully modified to include that it was subject to religious, ethnic, and other restrictions of member states.

Further testimony to this change of thinking occurred during a conversation I overheard between two delegates at the United Nations Fourth World Conference on Women in Beijing. A Sudanese delegate was engaged in an interesting conversation with a French delegate. Following are excerpts of the encounter:

> "Why are you so angry?" the Sudanese delegate asked. "You have all those rights you want us to accept — artificial birth control, sterilization, abortion, fetal experimentation, sex education from kindergarten on."
>
> "Because we want the whole world to have them," the French delegate responded.
>
> Then the Sudanese delegate asked: "But please show me a little window of your paradise, because you have all of these things and you are still not happy. All I see in your world is increased promiscuity among young people, increased divorce, increased abortion, homosexuality, venereal diseases in epidemic proportions. I don't see your paradise."
>
> The French delegate turned away in anger.

The delegate from the Sudan often referred to the western powers, saying: "Perhaps what is missing in the life-styles of the powerful leadership of the western nations is the belief in God? Hence their desire to impose their culture of death to the rest of the world. True happiness will not be found in liberating ourselves from nature and challenging God; our people are poor. All they have is their lifelong traditions and their religious beliefs that are in clear opposition to what they are trying to impose upon us."

In another tragic incident, the western delegates were trying to pass another dubious proposal entitled sexual rights. "Sexual rights!!" the Moroccan delegate exclaimed in exasperation at the insistence of the West to push programs and so-called rights that would not even be dreamed of by the poor of the world. "I have no idea what level of affluence you people are coming from, but our people need food, clean water, clothing, housing and you are fighting for 'sexual rights.' Can you imagine what my people would think if I go back to my country and tell them, I did not get you food, I did not get you water, I did not get you clothing or housing, but . . . I got you SEXUAL RIGHTS!!! They would think I had gone mad!"

Young people must be challenged

The inborn modesty and natural innocence of the young are being destroyed under the disguise of "sex education" without morals and values, totally excluding the rights of their parents.

As if this were not enough, proponents of the Platforms for Action insist that all methods of fertility control be made available to minors without parental consent or knowledge. Confidentiality is a cornerstone of their agenda and necessary, because when parents are forced out of the picture, those with a radical agenda and philosophy are empowered to fill in the gap.

Governments, schools, and universities here in the United States apparently hold to the fallacious ideology of throwing condoms, pills, and other technologies to boys and girls who, they presume, are incapable of living chaste lives. Isn't it time we challenge our younger generation to practice self control instead of birth control? Not only will it bring back respect and appreciation for the natural laws and the gift of fertility, but it will also serve as a remarkable teaching tool that will positively impact young people in many other areas of life. Only through this approach can we begin to reverse the shameful statistic that one in every five Americans has a sexually transmitted disease. This is largely because of the irresponsible promotion of birth control products by medical, academic, and government institutions. There is a better answer — a moral alternative that is proven to be extremely effective. It is based on the principle that parents are the primary influence in a child's life. The love, affection, and direction they give their children is the greatest deterrent against promiscuous behavior and other rebellious conduct often encountered in the adolescent years. It is a well-established fact that strong disciplined families produce more responsible citizens and, consequently, a better world.

It is a fact that everything we do in this life, good or bad, reflects back on us, our families and neighbors. For example, we must teach youngsters that if they are irresponsible and acquire a venereal disease by being promiscuous, the effect of their action falls on the whole community, starting with their parents, who must pay to cover the expense of their illness. If they are insured, the company will increase the cost of insurance to the whole community. If they don't have insurance, they must be cared for by the state, who in turn must increase everyone's taxes to cover the expense of their irresponsible behavior.

In our various engagements at the U.N. meetings, I asked the following questions of the western delegates:

- If the U.S. is presently experiencing an epidemic of sexually transmitted infections, with one of every five Americans infected, why are you proposing to export and expand failure to our developing countries?
- Wouldn't the addition of costly programs, especially programs that have failed in the richest nations of the world, increase the problems of the developing nations who are not equipped to handle them?

I repeatedly tried to make the delegates from the U.S. and other western countries understand that freedom without responsibility becomes anarchy, and that responsibility must be accompanied by self control. We do not want to turn our children into sexual addicts. Rather, we want to turn them into responsible parents and citizens.

Family of the Americas Foundation has an extraordinary and successful program directed toward parents of adolescents. Our program for parents was funded by a $1.2 million grant from the U.S. Department of Health and Human Services (HHS) from 1983-1987. This program for parents and adolescents promoted family-centered sexuality education, helping parents to assume their role as the principal educators of their children in matters of human sexuality.

By the end of the program, over six thousand parents and adolescents had been reached. The result of the program was an overall pregnancy rate of five per one thousand adolescent females, which was twenty-two percent lower than the national rate of one hundred eleven pregnancies per one thousand adolescent females. The evaluators concluded that the Family of the Americas program was successful in reaching a large number of participants of diverse ethnic origin, and that the program's benefits appear to be long-term in nature. The obvious success of our parent-centered sex education program received little publicity and no follow-up, presumably because it conflicted sharply with the politically powerful contraception lobby headed by Planned Parenthood.

The only way we are going to win is to teach couples to live in harmony with nature and respect God's laws through Natural Family Planning. We must also encourage and challenge young people to make the chastity pledge before they are exposed to a promiscuous life style. And for those who are no longer virgins, we offer the opportunity to return to a life of chastity.

Conclusion

In conclusion, I must admit that it is truly painful to associate ourselves with such U.N. documents, even on the basis of a "partial consensus," because it practically constitutes a form of material cooperation in the authorization of programs and policies that are going to be based on this (and previous) documents. With each "partial consensus," we are guilty of some form of "partial cooperation" with the forces intent on destroying our religious and cultural foundations. As this process continues and the "approved" documents' programs accumulate and expand, it becomes increasingly difficult to raise fundamental objections.

It seems ridiculous and unnatural to be fighting against our own people. Imagine the embarrassing example we are presenting to the world. Led by the U.S., the western countries, supposedly Christian, are the ones pushing for the legalization of abortion, worldwide population control, sex education without morals and values, the acceptance of homosexual practices, and much more. Countries rejecting such barbaric proposals, the countries standing up in defense of cultural morality, are the Moslems, some Hindus, and a sprinkling of Catholic countries from Latin America and Africa.

Nevertheless, any agreement made under coercion or duress must be considered illegal and nonbinding. It is on this basis that we have denounced the illegality of these conferences. The future of mankind is being decided by the anti-life/anti-family delegations, supported by the western governments, with total disregard for the culture, religion, and traditions of their own people and those of the developing world.

If we foresee the danger to our children, grandchildren, and the future of humanity, then we must join together to stop them. There are very few Davids willing to confront the Goliaths of this world. What is needed now is not words of praise and sympathy, but active support and voices raised in protest. We must stand up, speak out, and be counted.

The teachings of the Catholic Church have the answer. Let's work together for the good of our children and grandchildren. We do not want the poor countries of the world to have to barter their beliefs in exchange for food or loans, nor do we want to compromise our salvation by doing nothing.

The longer we delay our action in promoting family values, the harder it will be to reverse the damage. The time has come for leaders of the Catholic Church to be leaders, like the pope and Mother Teresa, for Catholics to be true Catholics, not cafeteria Catholics, selective of which commandments to follow and which to dismiss.

The future of humanity is in our hands. We must rescue the family from the tyranny of the United Nations. Our influence as parents and educators can defeat the forces of darkness. Let the forces of light be the shining stars for the future of humanity. The forces of good will triumph over the forces of evil only if we back up our words with action. It seems logical that in this great democracy, Catholics must support political candidates who support Christian morality and must oppose those who reject it. Inevitably, politics change policy.

Finally, I leave with you Mother Teresa's favorite prayer:

> *The fruit of silence is prayer.*
> *The fruit of prayer is faith.*
> *The fruit of faith is love.*
> *The fruit of love is service.*
> *The fruit of service is peace.*

Chapter XI
Helen M. Alvare

Abortion and the Culture of Death

While much has been written and said over decades about the twin assaults of abortion and euthanasia, nothing is as complete or as revealing as the papal encyclical, *Evangelium Vitae*, and the subsequent U.S. Catholic Bishops' statement, *Faithful for Life*. Especially for those who know little more about the Catholic Church's position on abortion and euthanasia than its opposition, these documents open up a world of understanding. The key to these documents, and therefore what lies at the very core of the Church's respect-life teachings, is through the metaphors first introduced by the pope himself, the "culture of death," versus the "culture of life."

"Today," the pope explains, new "threats to the life of individuals and peoples . . . are emerging on an alarming scale. . . . This reality is characterized by the emergence of a culture which denies solidarity and in many cases takes the form of a veritable 'culture of death.' This culture is actively fostered by powerful cultural, economic and political currents which encourage an idea of society excessively concerned with efficiency" *(Evangelium Vitae*, 3, 12).

The "culture of death" is a fairly dramatic term and claim. Are we really living, could it be possible to live, in a culture oriented toward death, not life? Isn't it a fundamental truism that each of us clings to life with tenacity? Aside from the rare siting of a "choose death" bumper sticker, have we ever heard anyone but the clinically depressed favoring death? Why would anyone want to choose what His Holiness calls the "culture of death"?

Living in a "culture of death"

In *Faithful for Life*, another powerful reflection on this same subject, the U.S. Catholic Bishops raise this same question from a different perspective: "How has it come to pass that the elimination of one's child or one's parent, acts of desperation wrought in every age, are now described as sensible and even attractive alternatives?" *(Faithful for Life*, p. 5). So often what we find is not that an individual, created by God, really wants death, but that some outside influence has been exerted to make that person think that his or her life is less than a life worth living. In today's society, that influence frequently comes from institutions, sometimes very powerful institutions, using their prestige to persuade people not that *they* should die, but that it might be better for *a certain person or a certain group of peopl*e to die. "A person who, because of illness, handicap or, more simply, just by existing, compromises the well-being or life-style of those who are more favored tends to be looked upon as an enemy to be resisted or eliminated" *(Evangelium Vitae*, 12). How often I have seen Planned Parenthood claim that it is cheaper for society if a woman chooses to have an abortion than to give birth to her child. And this is just one example.

Sadly, there is no denying that we are living in a culture of death, as understood to be a culture in which killing is around us, and is more and more proposed as a solution to problems. Our Holy Father points to a variety of evidence: the increasing presence of violence by individuals; the numbers of suffering children, often as a result of war or unjust distribution of resources; an out-of-control arms and drug trade; environmental abuse; and the spread of sexually transmitted disease *(Evangelium Vitae*, 10). "The Lord said to Cain: 'What have you done? The voice of your brother's blood is crying to me from the ground' (Genesis 4:10). *The voice of the blood shed by men continues to cry out*, from generation to generation, in ever new and different ways" *(Evangelium Vitae*, 10).

Most particularly, however, the pope points to abortion and euthanasia as signal evidence that we live in a culture of death. For it is in these practices that the most egregious elements of this deadly culture are found. In abortion and euthanasia, our society kills members of the human family when they are at their weakest—because of youth, age, disease, or disability. We kill in the name of "rights" and "freedom," sometimes even using subsidies from the state to pay for this killing. "[I]t is possible to speak in a certain sense of a *war of the powerful against the weak*: a life which would require greater acceptance, love and care is considered useless, or held to be an intolerable burden, and is therefore rejected in one way or another" (*Evangelium Vitae*, 11-12).

Most terrible and ironic, we kill *members of our own family.* In fact, as the bishops noted in *Faithful for Life*, it is *only* members of our immediate family that we can legally kill under our country's abortion and euthanasia regimes! This awful reality means that abortion and euthanasia not only destroy their victims, but reinforce the serious damage the family has sustained in today's society.

The family is the first haven [for] those who are dependent. . . . For this reason it can be called the "sanctuary of life" (*Evangelium Vitae*, 11). At the heart of this sanctuary is fidelity — unwavering loyalty both to those we choose and to those who have been given to us. The unraveling of that fidelity in our time leaves dependents to become lawful victims of their guardians.

The same shift towards the self has altered our society's views on marriage and divorce. . . . Christian marriage is the union of a man and a woman bound by the same transforming fidelity which Christ has for his Church: for better or worse. When a people lose confidence in fidelity between husbands and wives, it is an easy leap to imagine that other fidelities — of parents to children, and of adult children to their elder parents — no longer need to be permanent, for-better-or-for-worse obligations. . . . The home becomes the place where, when you knock, they no longer have to let you in *(Faithful for Life*, p. 6-7).

In addition to the individual practices of abortion and euthanasia, however, the pope notes how these practices are embraced by institutions on a worldwide basis to create veritable "structures of sin" (*Evangelium Vitae*, 12). Courts, organizations like the International Planned Parenthood Federation, and other institutions, are imbuing in society greater and greater bias toward the opinion that the value of all life is merely relative to its quality. That nothing like the "inherent dignity of the human person," exists. As *Faithful for Life* observes, "[abortion and euthanasia], proved through centuries of experience to be wrong and destructive of human life and human dignity, are in our day expounded upon in schoolrooms, prescribed by physicians, condoned by public figures, protected by courts, subsidized by legislatures, and even advertised in the Yellow Pages."

But what supports the structure of the "culture of death"? We would not have an abortion rate of 1.5 million abortions every year if enormous numbers of people and institutions had not accepted presuppositions which could lead them to the ultimate act of taking a defenseless child's life. "The Lord's question, 'What have you done?' which Cain cannot escape, is addressed also to the people of today, to make them realize the extent and gravity of the attacks against life which continue to mark human history . . ." (*Evangelium Vitae*, 10). As *Faithful for Life* expresses it: Abortion and euthanasia are "not the wayward gestures of the innocent; they are the forlorn acts of a society which has forgotten or rejected fidelity to its own. They are signs of a need for conversion."

Conversion from what? Our Holy Father says, conversion *first* from abuse of freedom to the practice of authentic freedom and *second* from forgetting God to remembering Him.

Freedom lost and abused

What passes for "freedom" today is one of the primary reasons why abortion persists in the United States. Freedom is falsely understood as a license to do whatever one wishes. "Free" of concern from the common good, and "free" of any allegiance to truth. The very ability to arbitrarily choose this thing instead of that, for any reason or no reason at all, is what passes for freedom. Freedom "ends up by becoming the freedom of 'the strong' against the weak who have no choice but to submit" (*Evangelium Vitae*, 19). That the result may be harm to another — even fatal harm — or an undermining of the natural law good is considered irrelevant. As the pope explains, "To claim the right to abortion, infanticide and euthanasia, and to recognize that right in law, means to attribute to human freedom a *perverse and evil significance*: that of an *absolute power over others and against others*. This is the death of true freedom: 'Truly, truly, I say to you, everyone who commits sin is a slave to sin' (John 8:34)" (*Evangelium Vitae*, 20).

Arguments for abortion proceed according to this fatal understanding of freedom. Abortion is deemed an exercise in "freedom of choice" simply because it is one among a number of pregnancy outcomes that a woman may wish to choose. That the child is killed and the woman is wounded; that abortion violates the natural processes of pregnancy and birth; that killing violates every human instinct and the truth about being human — these facts are definitionally excluded from this distorted notion of freedom. "Many in our society today," observe the U.S. Bishops in *Faithful for Life*:

> . . . seem to live by the belief that human beings find their ultimate sense and fulfillment in unlimited individual freedom. Unlimited personal choice is celebrated as the prerequisite for every satisfying human experience, even within the family. Yet such an individualistic concept of freedom severs the true meaning of freedom from its moorings and distorts social life. It extols a society in which individuals stand side by side, but have no bonds holding them together. Yet between life itself and freedom there is an inseparable bond, a link. And that link is love or fidelity. . ." (p. 8-9).

The dangers of forgetting God

Not surprisingly, it is also those who have "forgotten God" who are most likely to support abortion, to work to preserve its legality, and even to undergo it. While a strong belief in God, combined with the practice of a faith, are factors closely associated with a pro-life stance, their polar opposites are empirically associated with support for abortion, or with having received an abortion. Why? The answers are not complicated. When we forget who God is, we forget who we are. We forget that we — every human being — are created in God's image and likeness and that every single human being is therefore endowed with a unique dignity. "By living 'as if God did not exist,' man not only loses sight of the mystery of God, but also of the mystery of the world and the mystery of his own being" (*Evangelium Vitae*, 22). Along with this dignity comes the quality of inviolability. In other words, at the foundation of our human dignity is our right not to be violated, killed, by another. If we lose a sense of God, materialism becomes the norm, because only enjoying the present moment has meaning. And finally, in the absence of God, we lose a sense of sin. There is no transcendent, loving creator, who has established a way for us to live. Therefore there is no sin. "The values of *being* are replaced by those of *having*. The only goal which counts is the pursuit of one's own material well-being" (*Evangelium Vitae*, 23). To lose touch with God is to lose touch with the God who created us, who loves us, who knows us better than anyone else and who knows what it takes to make us happy. To lose touch with God is to lose a sense of who we are and to risk descending rapidly into chaos and barbarism.

In such a milieu, it is more than easy to understand how abortion and euthanasia take root. "In the materialistic perspective described so far, *interpersonal relations are seriously impoverished.* The first to be harmed are women, children, the sick or suffering, and the elderly. The criterion of personal dignity — which demands respect, generosity and service — is replaced by the criterion of efficiency, functionality and usefulness: others are considered not for what they 'are,' but for what the 'have, do and produce.' This is the supremacy of the strong over the weak" (*Evangelium Vitae*, 23).

This "culture of death" is completely antithetical to Gospel of Jesus Christ. "[I]s it not unthinkable," ask the bishops in *Faithful for Life*, "that people who call themselves Christians sometimes fit in so well among a people that tolerates the killing of its unborn children and elders?" (p. 5). "Abortion and euthanasia are thus crimes which no human law can claim to legitimize. There is no obligation in conscience to obey such laws; instead there is a *grave and clear obligation to oppose them by conscientious objection. . . . Individuals, families, groups and associations*, albeit for different reasons and in different ways, all have a responsibility for shaping society and developing cultural, economic, political and legislative projects which, with respect for all and in keeping with democratic principles, will contribute to the building of a society in which the dignity of each person is recognized and protected and the lives of all are defended and enhanced." (*Evangelium Vitae*, 73, 90).

Rebuilding the "culture of life"

The Holy Father knows that challenging the culture of death to renew the bonds of fidelity and love will not be easy; "There is," he says, "certainly an enormous disparity between the powerful resources available to the forces promoting the 'culture of death' and the means at the disposal of those working for a 'culture of life and love.' But we know that we can rely on the help of God, for whom nothing is impossible. . . . A *great prayer for life is urgently needed*, a prayer which will rise up throughout the world" (*Evangelium Vitae*, 100). And so he has asked us to begin this task with the following prayer:

> O Mary,
> bright dawn of the new world,
> Mother of the living,
> to you do we entrust the *cause of life*:
> Look down, O Mother,
> upon the vast numbers
> of babies not allowed to be born,
> of the poor whose lives are made difficult,
> of men and women
> who are victims of brutal violence,
> of the elderly and the sick killed
> by indifference or out of misguided mercy.
> Grant that all who believe in your Son
> may *proclaim the Gospel of life*
> with honesty and love
> to the people of our time.
> Obtain for them the grace
> to *accept that Gospel*
> as a gift ever new,
> the joy *of celebrating* it with gratitude
> throughout their lives and

the courage to *bear witness to it*
resolutely, in order to build,
together with all people of good will,
the civilization of truth and love,
to the praise and glory of God,
the Creator and lover of life.

Evangelium Vitae, 105

This antidote the pope prescribes for the situation known as the "culture of death," is, of course, the "culture of life." In such a culture, *ab initio*, God is "remembered," freedom is authentically exercised, and abortion is rejected, along with every violation of human life and authentic human freedom. In such a culture, the "Gospel of Life" — the way of Jesus Christ — is lived. At the very least, this means that each and every human person's right not to be killed is respected, without distinction according to age, size, gender, or any other quality. "True 'compassion' leads to sharing another's pain; it does not kill the person whose suffering we cannot bear" (*Evangelium Vitae*, 66). In fact, more than recognizing a right not to be killed on the part of vulnerable human like the elderly and unborn, we recognize a special duty towards them. Jesus exercised a "special option" for those in the greatest need. As the U.S. Bishops elaborated in *Faithful for Life*:

> We are all journeying down from Jerusalem to Jericho, and [the Good Samaritan] story haunts us, for it flatly contradicts the strong persuasion so widely held today that our loyalties and our obligations are owed only to those of our choice. On the contrary, we owe fidelity to those we choose and, beyond them, to others we do not choose. It is *we* who have been chosen to go out of our way for them.

> The core work of building the culture of life is therefore none other than evangelization. Before many will be able to reach the conclusion that abortion is wrong, they need to be converted to certain truths about God and about human freedom. If such a conversion of culture took place,

abortion would be unthinkable. Until it does, abortion — and a host of other violations of human life — will seem not only logical, but almost inevitable, to many.

A Growing Consensus: Choice in Education

One of the most dynamic and fundamental roles parents play in the lives of their children is that of teacher, educating them academically, morally, and socially. The *Catechism of the Catholic Church* states that "parents have the first responsibility for the education of children" (2223) and that "as those first responsible for the education of their children, parents have the right to choose a school for them which corresponds to their own convictions. This is fundamental. . . . Public authorities have the duty of guaranteeing this parental right and of ensuring the concrete conditions for its exercise" (2229). While recent societal demands have pressured many parents into relinquishing some of the control over their children's education to others, any constriction of educational opportunity violates the civil and religious rights of the family.

Historically, family involvement and community participation have formed the foundation of the education system in the United States. However, in the past thirty years, control of our public schools has ebbed from local communities and flowed toward centralized, multilevel bureaucracies. David Boaz and R. Morris Barrett of the Cato Institute report the number of nonteaching bureaucrats mushroomed 500 percent from 1960 to 1984 in America's public schools. The U.S. now spends about $15 billion, a quarter of its total education budget, on nonteaching personnel.

As government's role in education has waxed, the role of parents and families has waned. Some argue that this encroachment has occurred because the definition of the traditional family has changed and that the state has found it necessary to step in to fill the vacuum. While this contention contains an element of truth, we now must focus on the reforms necessary to give parents greater control over their children's education.

History — how did we get here?

The burgeoning of the welfare state and the "War on Poverty" perverted U.S. education policy. In the 1960s, government leaders decided that part of the cause of poverty was inadequate education, and therefore began to take a more active role in the formulation and funding of educational programs. Begun in the Department of Health, Education and Welfare, education policy was later spun-off under the specialized Department of Education.

Yet this bureaucracy soon sprawled out of control, importing armies of administrators into each new level of government oversight. As federal funding for these programs ballooned, the focus on education was lost.

When studying Chicago's public schools for the *Chicago Tribune*, Bonita Brodt found "an institutionalized case of child neglect . . . the misplaced priorities of a centralized school bureaucracy, and the vested interests of a powerful teachers (sic) union had all . . . taken precedence over the needs of the very children the schools are supposed to serve." Steve Jobs, founder of Apple Computers, adds "I've had to come to the inevitable conclusion that the problem is not one technology can hope to solve. . . . It's a political problem. . . ."

Present — a choice alternative

Fortunately, the Catholic school system in this country, especially in many of our urban areas, is both extensive and accomplished. Schools run by religious orders and parishes have thrived because parents and families recognize the academic and religious values these schools instill. Many such inner-city Catholic schools serve a majority of non-Catholic, racial, and ethnic minorities, providing direction, moral guidance, and structure to communities and children who may come from broken families or other challenging life-situations.

Nora Basey, a single grandmother, spends half her salary on tuition for her grandson at Archbishop John Carroll High School in Washington, D.C. "Everything I make I put to the school. . . . You wonder how I eat. . . . But it's worth it in the end, just to see him out there learning to be independent," she says.

Families like the Baseys value the benefits of schools like Archbishop Carroll, and pay tuition willingly, if not easily. "It is almost painful to see some of the sacrifices our families make to send their children here," laments Carroll's development director Father John Mudd.

Nevertheless, the issue is not how to help Catholic schools, but how to help children. The real issue is how to give *all* parents the opportunity to provide their child with a solid education. Without access to realistic options to the public school system, poor families are too often forced to send their children to inferior schools. In the "I Have a Dream Program" conducted in the South Bronx, for instance, students were offered college tuition if they successfully completed high school. One benefactor, who "adopted" a public high school class and a Catholic high school class, saw two out of thirty-eight of his public school students go on to college and twenty out of twenty-two Catholic school students. "They were the same kids from the same families and the same housing projects," the benefactor observed. "In fact, sometimes one child went to public school and a sibling went to Catholic school. We even gave money to the public school kids for tutoring and after-school programs. It's just that the Catholic schools worked and the others didn't."

That's why Karren Walker and Zaneta Simms, two single mothers from Washington, D.C., used these words to ask Congress for the right to school choice: "Every day, DC kids have to face violence, drugs, gangs and guns at school. They deserve a better chance. They passed a bill in Congress to create a scholarship program for the kids of low income parents. Like our kids. The bill would let our kids go to any school. Just like President Clinton's daughter does."

An issue of religious liberty

Parents' rights to educational choice isn't just a right to provide the best economic opportunities for their children, but a basic moral right with much broader implications. Educational choice reflects traditional Catholic values. The *Catechism*, as shown above, views the right of parents to choose their children's schools as a fundamental right (2223, 2229). Pope John Paul II stresses that, "Parents have the

123

right to choose schools or other means necessary to educate their children in keeping with their convictions. Public authorities must ensure that public subsidies are so allocated that parents are truly free to exercise that right without incurring unjust burdens" (*Charter of the Rights of the Family*).

Catholic Americans also support school choice because it protects the family from state interference into private and religious matters. Most countries around the world safeguard their families from educational intrusion by providing school choice programs to their citizens. In Canada and Australia, governments make direct payment to schools based on their class size regardless of their private or public status. Current school choice programs also enjoy broad-based support from families in France and Germany. And in Belgium and Holland, school choice is so popular that a majority of parents use government money to send their children to private schools. Yet in none of these countries has the academic excellence of the public schools ever been questioned or undermined by the right of parents to send their children to private schools.

In our country, however, parents fear that public schools will ridicule their family's beliefs rather than respect them. Parents in New York City protested for months against public school authorities who insisted on including *Heather Has Two Mommies* in the grade school curriculum. Parents were forced to organize substantial political pressure to finally have their rights recognized. Far too many parents have faced school boards all too willing to distribute condoms to children their parents felt were too young, immature, or ill-prepared to deal with the explosive issues involved. Sandy Martinez, a parent in Chelmsford, Massachusetts, reports her daughter was forced to attend safe-sex classes in school or face detention. School choice ameliorates arguments over religious and moral differences by allowing parents to choose the schools which best reflect and respect their family's values.

Obstacles to educational choice

Opponents of these policies have a range of reasons why school choice will not or can not work. The first is separation of church and state, that public tax dollars should not subsidize religious institutions. The fact is the present system merely discriminates against students from the first through twelfth grades. Government aid helps finance college for students attending Notre Dame and Yeshiva as well as preschool for kids attending public or private institutions; only primary and secondary school students do not enjoy this benefit.

Others object that school choice will destroy the public school system. The fact is that public schools can compete and that school choice will only give the public system a much-needed incentive to improve. One example of a public system that competes is Community School District #4 in New York City. Located in the neighborhood of lower-income East Harlem, it tailors its curriculum to the needs of the low-income families it serves. There is no junior high; rather parents and students choose from among schools that combine a base curriculum with a chosen specialization. Despite its Harlem address, District #4 (one of thirty-two New York City elementary school districts) receives several applications from students who attend much wealthier private schools outside the ghetto. The success of District #4 proves schools that meet the needs of their students can and will survive.

Conclusion

The main political opposition for these policies comes from those who have helped to build the education bureaucracy that currently runs the public schools. While a plurality of public school teachers send their children to private schools (over fifty percent in urban municipalities), the defenders of the public school system continue to block initiatives that would expand options for many confined to public schools. Understandably concerned about protecting the quality of public school education, the leaders of the educational bureaucracy have mistakenly concluded it necessary to vigorously oppose school choice in order to save public schools. They have therefore resolved to smother opportunities for the less fortunate to obtain an education for their children anywhere outside of the public school domain. Until workable school choice plans provide viable alternatives, these leaders will occupy key ground from which to defend the bureaucracies they have built and to attack school choice. With the power of choice in the hands of parents, however, public school boards will enjoy the freedom and motivation to create and innovate. They will be able to downsize bureaucracy rather than bow down before it and improve both the private *and* the public school options available to all children.

Expanding opportunities, like the D.C. initiative, for the poor and all American families expels discrimination and empowers parents to educate their children as they see fit. School choice provides parents with the essential tools to both provide their children with the best opportunities and to have authority over their children's moral formation. Whether this is in the public school system, in a private or parochial school, or home-schooling, all options must be made available to all parents. Tuition tax credits, tax-funded scholarships, and voucher programs return power to parents, decentralize bloated bureaucracies, and make quality schools affordable and available to all. In a pilot program last year, twelve private schools in Milwaukee were allowed to enroll sixty-five percent of their students with M.P.C.P. (Milwaukee Parental Choice Program) vouchers. Though challenged by its opponents in court, this initiative enjoys a ninety-five percent approval rating from Milwaukee parents. There is no reason why all of America's families and students should not be similarly satisfied with their educational opportunities.

Chapter XIII
Congressman Christopher Smith

Judeo-Christian Values in Politics, Media, and Culture

Organizations like the Catholic Campaign for America are the hope for mobilizing our Catholic brothers and sisters to be — as our Lord said in the Gospel — as wise as serpents, yet gentle as doves. This message, a message from Christ, is one we must take to heart, especially in the public square, in order to ensure that the innocent and disenfranchised in our society are protected.

Indeed, over the years, there have been too few soldiers willing to stand up, to jump in, and to fight to make the difference. The only thing necessary for evil to triumph over good is for good men and good women to do nothing — or only a little bit. As uncomfortable as it might be, we have a responsibility to take on evil in the public square as St. Paul said, to fight the good fight, and to persevere as to win.

Moral standards in our society have been declining for decades, and the Church, both laity and clergy, have been like salt slowing the decay. Yet, corrosion has taken place and we have our work cut out for us. Unfortunately, "trash talk," sexual promiscuity, and the portrayal of moral indecisiveness in television, movies, and popular literature have all increased. We are swimming against a very heavy tide. As St. Paul remarks, we are fighting against spiritual forces that we cannot physically see.

It is my hope that society has reached its darkest hour and that evil's temporary advances will be paralyzed. I am hopeful that enough people have been awakened to the evil in our midst and are prepared to rededicate themselves to reestablishing moral standards in society. The Houseof Representative's vote to override the president's veto of the partial-birth abortion ban is just one example of what we can accomplish when we join together for a just and moral cause.

The partial-birth abortion ban act

Even though the partial-birth abortion ban act was a very modest piece of legislation, outlawing only one method of abortion, this vote was a great victory for the pro-life movement and unborn children. Let us remember that all abortions, including partial-birth abortions, are horrific and "extreme." The other methods of abortion such as chemical poisonings with salt solutions, dismemberment by way of suction machine and knives, and D&E which, literally, decapitates and takes off the arms and legs of unborn babies, are no less painful to the child. But it was this vote, the vote to ban partial-birth abortions, which helped the American public to refocus on the fact that, by their very nature, abortions, all abortions, are horrible to contemplate.

And it was the partial-birth abortion ban legislation which helped expose the dirty, little secret that "abortion kills children."

For twenty-four years society has lived in denial. The slick euphemisms of the abortion industry have moved the focus off the violence of abortion. Abortion is not benign as the word "choice" implies. No, abortion is the worst kind of violence. Violence against children and violence against women as well.

We all know women who have had abortions. I personally know more than a dozen women who have had abortions. They are the co-victims of an industry bent on making money — regardless of the pain and torture perpetrated on an innocent unborn child and a mother in crisis.

There are people who have been inside the abortion industry — such as Dr. Carol Everett and Dr. Bernard Nathanson — who performed abortions but have now rejected the horror of the industry. Having worked within, they can now tell us that the real story of abortion clinics is a matter of dollars and cents. It is an industry predicated on greed and death.

Abortion is also a symbol of the so-called "sexual revolution" which promotes radical individualism and sexual promiscuity without regard to the children. In this way, abortion is seen as an acceptable "last resort" to shield people from their own irresponsibility. This kind of cynicism is part of the decline of moral standards in our society.

The vote on the partial-birth abortion ban finally put into perspective what it is that we are really talking about when we debate abortion. The media tends to emphasize all of the "hard" stories. Yes, there are hard cases, but they are diversionary. They are few and they have — until now — steered the debate away from the reality that each and every abortion takes the life of a living child, harms the mother, and adds to the decay of our society.

The pro-abortion side has been distorting the real story and professing the so-called "right" to abortion so it may continue unfettered. But the debate over partial-birth abortion has revealed their deception. For the first time ever, the pro-life position was being understood. A few news columnists and some members of Congress (with one-hundred percent Planned Parenthood voting records) started writing and saying that pro-abortionists were going too far. They were telling others about the reality of partial-birth abortion — that a child three-fourths of the way born has the back of his head pierced with scissors so that his brain can be evacuated and extracted by way of suction machine. It is criminal, and many pro-abortion legislators saw this for the first time.

In fact, during the debate, one speaker after another, Democrats and Republicans, took to the podium and called it, "child abuse." While the House voted to override President Clinton's veto of the ban, the Senate did not.

Bill Clinton: pro-abortion extremist

It is a national tragedy that Bill Clinton, alone with his veto pen stood in the way of the partial-birth abortion ban. Yet, it was not totally unexpected.

President Bill Clinton has signaled his extremism on abortion many times during his administration. Four years ago, many of us knew that he was pro-abortion. We were scared as to what he would do and every single, solitary fear of ours has been realized. Fortunately, the Republicans of the 104th Congress and the pro-life Democrats blocked some of President Clinton's pro-abortion initiatives and repealed others. There are many.

Specifically, through the "Freedom of Access to Clinic Entrances" law, President Clinton has turned nonviolent Americans who say rosaries in front of abortion clinics into felons. What this means is that if you try to reach out to a woman with a positive, nonviolent alternative or to say "please reconsider," you may be charged under federal laws and convicted as a federal criminal.

This is purely dictatorial, with a small "d" of course, because we still have due process. But the bottom line is that the law mandates punitive damages and up to two years in jail for anyone who was simply trying to reason with a woman on her way into an abortion mill and to stop the abortion about to take place. The Clinton law has fostered a "throw the book at 'em" attitude without true justice. If you were to protest in front of that abortion mill and say you want higher wages or better working conditions inside of that mill, there is no federal penalty. But if your intention is to try to save an innocent baby and a victimized mother, you will face penalties instituted by an increasingly two-tiered, discriminatory legal framework.

Let us not forget the Freedom of Choice Act of 1993, which Bill and Hillary Clinton so regularly advocated. Everyone forgets, including myself, that this legislation was written by Planned Parenthood and the National Abortion Rights Action League (NARAL). Many modest state laws restricting abortion-on-demand, such as waiting periods and woman's right to know laws, which allow women — prior to the irreversible decision of the abortion — to know what the child looks like, would have been overturned by Clinton's Freedom of Choice Act. The Freedom of Choice Act of 1993 would have nullified all of the modest restrictions on abortion-on-demand so that the woman remains uninformed and pressured to have an abortion.

In addition to pushing the Freedom of Choice Act, Bill Clinton, through his radical health care plan, was also pushing for an abortion mandate that would have forced every HMO, every hospital, and every access point for health care to perform or refer for abortions. He wielded incredible pressure on hospitals and managed care institutions to go along with the mandate. Fortunately, he was defeated.

But we haven't been able to stop his push for the new baby

poison known as RU-486. On his second day in office, he put the Department of Health on notice that he wanted an expedited approval of RU-486 despite its known side-effects. The very fact that RU-486 has been sponsored by the Population Council ought to send up some alarm bells. Planned Parenthood is right there side-by-side with them trying to bring this new means of destroying innocent babies to our shores and further privatize the killing of unborn babies. And that's just the beginning. The grand plan is that once RU-486 is approved by the U.S. Food and Drug Administration, the abortion industry will just roll it out to other countries who will believe that if it's approved in America, it ought to be safe for them as well.

Clinton administration exports abortion

One of the things that my work on the International Relations Committee gives me is a perspective on how incredibly well-situated the United States is — how respected we are — especially in the fields of health and medicine. If the U.S. thinks something is okay, there is an almost automatic acceptance by other countries, particularly by their health ministers. Now if the FDA, with its normally vigorous regiment for approving drugs, says, as it is in the process of doing, that RU-486 (the baby poison) is just great, that will be the green light around the world. This is precisely why the Population Council, which says it believes there are just too many of us, wants a "fast-track" approval of RU-486 from the Clinton administration. They want to put the FDA's stamp of approval on this very dangerous baby poison, so they can export it and ram it down the throats of women in other countries. So not only do we get it here, but it has the twin shame of also being exported—and our president is the villain who is giving it that massive push out the door.

Then there is this administration's obsession, and I can't underscore that word enough, with exporting abortion to the countries of the world where the unborn are protected. Virtually all the countries of Central and South America (with the exception of Cuba) as well as the African countries and Ireland and the Philippines all protect the lives of their unborn children from almost every abortion — it's in their constitutions. And yet the Clinton administration is providing our international foreign aid dollars to population control groups that work very hard, with a zest and zeal I have never seen before, to have these laws overturned.

The Clinton administration wants to provide the foreign aid money to nongovernmental organizations without any strings. Massive amounts of money go to population control organizations that use abortion as a method of family planning, as if they have an entitlement. We're trying to stop it and require that money be granted only on the condition that they stop performing and promoting abortion. Instead, under Clinton's free money program, these groups are busy undermining pro-life laws in their host countries. For instance, groups like Planned Parenthood set up shop in Lima and in Brazil and they lobby against pro-life laws. They get the health ministers working with them and they supply host countries with bogus data on abortions and on why they need to "liberalize" their law.

It has already happened. Look at Poland, where they recently reversed a law that protected their unborn babies. Planned Parenthood sees it as its mission — I have their documents and there is nothing hidden about this — to tear down pro-life laws wherever they exist. When they talk to Congressmen, they talk about contraception only. But in their own documents and in the day-to-day work of their family planning organizations in country X, Y, or Z, they stress their plans to bring down the pro-life laws. They emphasize the hard cases, they talk about the "large numbers" of women who died from illegal abortions, and they absolutely exaggerate it.

Their numbers and their data are not credible. In this country, they used to say that ten thousand women die every year from illegal abortion. Dr. Nathanson was one of those who crafted or helped to craft that number. He has told us, and former Surgeon General Dr. Coop has told us, that's absolute nonsense. We know that before *Roe* v. *Wade*, some women died from illegal abortion and that's not good — you want to stop it. But now women still die from legal abortion, as do their children, and we shouldn't forget that.

The numbers they used to excite us were untrue, exaggerated deliberately in order to get the public's sympathy. And now they are exaggerating in every capital of the world to get pro-life laws changed. And the U.S., through the policies of the abortion President Bill Clinton, is subsidizing this effort. His people, like Tim Wirth, undersecretary for global affairs, an absolute "dyed-in-the-wool" pro-abortionist, goes into these capitals using the strength of our vast bureaucracy, which includes all of our embassies, to try to bring down these pro-life laws. He pressures recipient countries with talk of population control and demands for in-country programs to curb their growth.

Right before the Conference on Population was held in Cairo, under the auspices of the United Nations, a cable was sent out by the U.S. government to key officials in our embassies that said that the U.S. would be pushing at Cairo for an international right to abortion. I was on "Meet the Press" with Al Gore from Cairo, and he denied it flatly. But we had a copy of the cable in black and white. And beyond that, everything that the official U.S. delegation did at that conference with the text of the document was in support of abortion-on-demand. Even when Clinton and Gore and their delegation publicly backed away from using the "absolute right for abortion" verbiage, they still worked behind the scenes and tried every which way to backdoor the so-called right to abortion into the conference document.

It was, as you know, the Holy See, working with the Central and South Americans, that stopped most of that mischief from going forward. We, as Catholics, can be very proud of the Holy See, which sent extremely effective diplomats and had a lot of caring, dedicated people networked in Cairo accurately exposing what the U.S. — that is, Clinton — was trying to do. As Americans, we must be ashamed of our president and his administration's fixation on abortion-on-demand around the globe.

It is frightening what the Clinton administration is trying to do. Just consider this: UNICEF, the United Nation's children's fund, is an organization that is supposed to be a frontline defender for children against disease and death. I am the chairman of the Subcommittee on International Operations and Human Rights and, as

133

such, maintain prime jurisdiction over the U.S. contributions to the UNICEF budget. The U.S. gives UNICEF about one hundred million dollars per year.

But we have a situation now where we have at the helm of UNICEF a woman by the name of Carol Bellamy. Those here from New York remember her quite well. Not only is she strongly pro-abortion, but when Ms. Bellamy was in the New York State Senate, she voted against a bill that would have provided for a standard of care for any child who survives a later term abortion. In other words, the bill would have required that if a child survives an abortion and hangs onto life, crying and kicking, you must provide the same standard of care that you would have provided had that child been born prematurely. Pretty modest stuff in my view. But Carol Bellamy voted against that bill.

This extremist of the culture of death is now, at the lobbying behest of Bill and Hillary Clinton, the head of UNICEF. And every time we turn around, people on the UNICEF board — Bellamy, the Netherlands' and Norway delegations — are trying to push abortion. They're trying to push population control as part of their basic services. It's perverse.

So in addition to the mischief of the U.N. Population Fund, we now have to be watching UNICEF every single hour of every single day. They may already be working hand-in-glove with the population control lobbyists, for all we know, because they often try to hide from us a lot of what they do. But believe me, as chairman, I monitor every U.S. dollar as closely as possible.

Right now, who is going to head the U.N. is another huge concern on the international front. The head of the U.N. is extremely powerful. For example, the U.N. Secretary General has incredible influence over developing countries of the world. The U.N. Secretary General decides what kind of help to give to what countries through the U.N.'s specialized agencies. The U.N. chief also helps countries get access to credit and funding from the World Bank and the International Monetary Fund. Thus, when the U.N. speaks, a lot of these developing countries do listen with very attentive ears.

U.N. Secretary General Boutros Boutros Ghali, whose term is expiring, is opposed by the Clinton administration for another term. He may still get another term — if other countries support him. He is at least nominally pro-life, or so he says. Very seldom does he follow through on pro-life initiatives. But there are some people who are in the mix that would be worse. They would be abortion advocates and would push a pro-abortion agenda on unsuspecting leaders and vulnerable children around the world.

Prime Minister Brotland from Norway and President Mary Robinson from Ireland, who are stridently pro-abortion, have been mentioned as candidates. Prime Minister Brotland gave a speech in Cairo and she called for an international "right" to abortion. All the other social issues that very often go like a train behind such a pro-abortion agenda constitute her vision of where the world ought to be going.

I raised this issue of the nomination of the next U.N. leader at a hearing with then Secretary of State Warren Christopher. I assured him I will do everything in my power to take away U.S. contributions to the U.N. if the Clinton administration has a role in putting either of these two or any other like-minded, strident, left-of-center pro-abortionists at the helm of the U.N.

In addition to raising this issue at congressional hearings, I wrote an op-ed for *Earth Times* (the newspaper of record for the United Nations) pointing out the problem with pro-abortion nominees. In response, they printed a letter from the Zero Population Growth (ZPG) group. Some of you who are from Pennsylvania know that former Congressman Peter Kostmeyer now heads ZPG. In Congress, he was obsessed with pushing the abortion agenda. His letter in response to mine exposed ZPG's worldwide push for abortion-on-demand. And believe me, this group and other population control groups have a lot of power. If you give them the money — without conditions — they could do a tremendous amount of damage to innocent children, to the family, and to everything we believe in.

Catholics must pray, fast, and work for traditional family values

I really believe that as Catholics, if we don't become proactive, our federal money will be used to pay for abortion. Now

I may be painting somewhat of a bleak picture because we have had twenty-five floor fights this Congress on abortion. But so far throughout my sixteen years in Congress, the pro-abortion forces have tried every year to pay for abortions through various appropriations bills.

The pro-abortion lobby, including President Clinton, wants to use our tax dollars to pay for abortions in the federal employee health benefits plans, in military hospitals, and in federal prisons. They want Congress to permit public funds to be used to pay for abortions in the District of Columbia. These are some of the battles we won in the 104th Congress, but they will be fought again.

As men and women of faith, we are at a crisis point, perhaps as never before. The commodity called Bill Clinton is well-known and defined now. We've got to penetrate and expose the myth that he wants abortions to be "rare." His every action in this regard has contradicted that statement.

Bill Clinton is the master chameleon — he can deceive like no one I have ever seen before, and I have been in politics a lot of years. He is very good at it. And when you have people like Governor Casey and the forty-five or so House Democrats who speak honestly and forthrightly and out of conviction, and who work hard to protect unborn children and defend moral values, it shows that the Democrat party can find its soul again. But it won't, as long as Bill Clinton is at the helm.

I know as a group, the Catholic Campaign for America can't advocate a particular candidate for president. But you — the individual members — can and must work hard to ensure that others know the power and the consequences of their votes. And you must work hard to emphasize the need for Catholics to vote on the social issues.

I look at the poll data released by the Catholic Campaign for America. There is some good news in it but there is also some very disturbing news. The poll shows the apathy of our Catholic people. It shows Catholics not caring about basic, fundamental moral issues, but caring only about issues that affect our wallets and our pocketbooks.

If this is the case, then we really have lost our vision and we have yielded to the secular influences of a modern age. We need to awaken that soul that is a slumbering giant right now.

No matter who wins our elections, I just ask you to redouble your own efforts in the fight for life and the fight for traditional family values. No matter who wins, we must pray and fast that our nation's leaders do the right thing. And I mean pray as we have never prayed before. Pray and work as if our own lives depended upon it, because the future of our nation certainly does.

Index

Our Sunday Visitor...
Your Source for Discovering the Riches of the Catholic Faith

Our Sunday Visitor has an extensive line of materials for young children, teens, and adults. Our books, Bibles, booklets, CD-ROMs, audios, and videos are available in bookstores worldwide.

To receive a FREE full-line catalog or for more information, call **Our Sunday Visitor** at **1-800-348-2440**. Or write, **Our Sunday Visitor** / 200 Noll Plaza / Huntington, IN 46750.

- -

Please send me: __ A catalog
Please send me materials on:
   __ Apologetics and catechetics   __ Reference works
   __ Prayer books   __ Heritage and the saints
   __ The family   __ The parish

Name_____
Address_____Apt._____
City_____State__Zip_____
Telephone ( )_____
A73BBABP

- -

Please send a friend: __ A catalog
Please send a friend materials on:
   __ Apologetics and catechetics   __ Reference works
   __ Prayer books   __ Heritage and the saints
   __ The family   __ The parish

Name_____
Address_____Apt._____
City_____State__Zip_____
Telephone ( )_____
A73BBABP

- -

Our Sunday Visitor
200 Noll Plaza
Huntington, IN 46750
1-800-348-2440
OSVSALES@AOL.COM

Your Source for Discovering the Riches of the Catholic Faith